Contents

Introduction

The Domesday Book has always intrigued its readers. To contemporaries, its exhaustive nature and the very finality of its written evidence made it resemble an apocalyptic last judgement. To more recent readers, its value lies in the picture it gives us of English society on the eve of the Norman Conquest, and again twenty years later. It is a picture which owes its fascination not only to the wide scope of its canvas, but also to its wealth of detail. We enjoy looking into Domesday in the way that we enjoy acting as spectators to the bustling crowd scenes of a painting by Breughel.

For teachers, Domesday forms a valuable resource for class assignment work. Not only is there the opportunity to see what was going on in our own town or village 900 years ago – how many people lived there, what sort of farming was carried out; there is also the opportunity for pupils to acquire and practise the data-handling skills of collation, comparison and analysis. Domesday Book can also profitably be fitted into its political and cultural context. It was, after all, one of the most important achievements of the Norman conquerors, who had landed so successfully at Hastings only 20 years before. Anglo-Saxon culture was rich and sophisticated; many examples survive of its literature and art. The Normans themselves built many churches, castles and cathedrals which can still be admired today.

This book aims to help the teacher who is interested in using Domesday Book in the classroom to make the fullest possible use of the available material. It starts with a brief description of Domesday Book; what it contains and why it was compiled. Then information is presented about how to find the translated text of the Domesday entries for your own locality. This is followed by a sample interpretation of the Domesday description of one village, with a discussion of some of the more problematic Domesday vocabulary and a glossary. Various suggestions for classroom work are then put forward, together with a short anthology of contemporary prose and poetry. Finally, a 'how to find out more' section contains annotated bibliographies of books for teachers and children, lists of readily-available filmstrips, records and posters, and suggestions for places to visit.

The Normans and Domesday Book

What is Domesday Book?

What is known as Domesday Book is actually *two* substantial volumes, one considerably larger than the other, called Great and Little Domesday respectively. (See p. 9 for *why* there are two volumes.) They contain, between them, the results of a massive survey, or inquest, undertaken in 1086 on the orders of William the Conqueror, into the state of his recently-conquered kingdom. The information they contain is minutely detailed, and gives not only the names of all the major landowners in the kingdom, but also the size and value of their estates, and a description of the number and condition of the ordinary people of the country who were bound, by a variety of obligations, to these great lords. Woods, pasture, livestock, watermills, ploughs and sometimes churches are detailed, and the value of each estate to its lord and for taxation purposes is also given.

King William was anxious to know (and modern historians have been grateful to learn) how things had changed in the countryside since 1066, when he had conquered the land. Each manor was meant to be described at the time of the Conquest, at the time it was granted as a reward to one of the Conqueror's Norman followers, and then at the time of the Domesday inquiry in 1086, although this did not always happen.

Within each volume, entries are arranged by counties according to the following format. First the lord of a group of manors, or estates, is named. This could be the King himself or someone who held his lands directly from him. Next, the name of the individual manor, and that of the 'hundred', or subdivision of a county, in which the estate was situated, is given. If the manor had been leased to a sub-tenant, or farmer, then his name follows. Then the name of the village, or other settlement, is given. Since a very large proportion of England's population lived and worked in the countryside at the time of Domesday Book, most entries relate to village life. The manor is then described; details of the land, its inhabitants and their livestock given. Its value and its liability to pay tax are noted. Finally, any miscellaneous information, or the existence of any disputes about ownership, is recorded. Entries relating to towns are of rather variable quality, and less standardised.

The two Domesday volumes were the end result of a very thorough and complex investigative process. This is described in greater detail on pp. 8–9.

The volumes were written out by royal scribes based at the king's treasury at Winchester, where they remained for several centuries. They are now kept in the Public Record Office, Chancery Lane Branch, London, where they will be on display during 1986.

Generations of historians have been fascinated by Domesday Book, and the text of each volume has been closely studied and hotly debated for hundreds of years. The following chapter attempts briefly to summarise their views, and to describe current historical thinking as to how and why Domesday Book was drawn up. The booklists on pp. 42–43 offer suggestions for further reading on these detailed topics.

The Norman Conquest

1066 is probably the best-known date in English history. It records not only the humiliating defeat of the English King Harold by the Norman Duke William but also the introduction of many new and significantly different features into English society. By 1086, only twenty years after the Conquest, when Domesday Book was compiled, many changes had taken place in England. A new dynasty of kings – William's English title, the 'Conqueror' (in Normandy he had been known as William the Bastard), says it all – had been established. A new, foreign, aristocracy had almost entirely replaced the pre-Conquest Anglo-Saxon ruling class. By 1086, Domesday records only two major landowners as being English. All the rest were Norman or French. It was the same for the Church. Norman bishops and abbots were introduced to replace the old Anglo-Saxon intelligentsia. All these new men brought with them a new language, French, which replaced Old English as the spoken language of government and the written language of literature. Even though it did not manage to wipe out English completely as the language of ordinary people, it introduced many changes into the language, and many telling new words, too. English farmworkers looked after cows, sheep and swine in the fields, but their Norman masters ate beef, mutton and pork at great feasts in their new castles and manor houses.

Modern historians have examined the precise effects of the Conquest in the spheres of government, administration, and social and economic change, in considerable detail. The old view, that the Normans made a clean break with the Anglo-Saxon past in 1066, and introduced many characteristically 'feudal' institutions, such as castles, or mounted knights, or bureaucratic government, has given way to a picture of less dramatic change. William the Conqueror is revealed not so much as an energetic innovator, sweeping away all the vestiges of the old Anglo-Saxon state, but as a skilful exploiter of much that was most useful and efficient in its governmental machine. The Anglo-Saxon monarchy had ruled England with the help of a council of noblemen; there was a professional royal secretariat; kings made their instructions known by sending out detailed written instructions, known as 'writs'; the countryside was divided into counties, or shires, each with a resident royal official, the shire-reeve (sheriff); many of the government's expenses were funded by a system of taxation known as 'geld'. All these continued after the Conquest, and formed the framework for King William's administration. It has even been suggested that Domesday Book itself was based in part on pre-Conquest documents recording the obligations of various lords to pay tax on their estates.

In spite of this continuity, there can be no doubt that the Norman Conquest did bring about substantial changes. As well as the changeover of men at the top of the social pyramid, there were also changes in status among the ordinary people. Slavery had been allowed in Anglo-Saxon society. Pre-conquest lords of manors had worked their estates with slaves, who had been their personal property, and who had been fed and housed by the lords. There were other tenants living and working on the lords' estates, and performing labour services for them, but these had been free men in the eyes of the law. Many Anglo-Saxon tenants had even been free to transfer their political allegiance from one lord to another, taking their land with them. Twenty years after the Conquest, we can see in Domesday Book that the status of many of these ordinary people had fallen. There were fewer slaves, certainly, but in many parts of the country, some of the lower ranks of tenants had become more firmly bound to their lords, and were probably paying higher rents or performing a greater number of labour services than their forebears had done.

The psychological effect of the Conquest must not be ignored, either. Without doubt, the new ruling class was resented, and there were several unsuccessful rebellions, led by members of the old aristocracy, against the new Norman lords. William the Conqueror repressed these with considerable savagery. Evidence of this 'scorched earth' policy can be seen in some of the Domesday entries. Contemporary writers also felt the shame of the Conquest deeply. The *Anglo-Saxon Chronicle*, a monastic history of England started in the 10th century and continued for many years after 1066, was in no doubt as to the effects of the Conquest. Its final entry for the year 1066 ends with a description of the Norman occupying army who 'built castles far and wide throughout the land, oppressing the wretched people and bringing things from bad to worse'.

The Decision to Compile Domesday Book

The *Anglo-Saxon Chronicle* also records King William's decision to compile Domesday Book (the full text of this entry is given on p. 36). 1085 had been a dangerous year for William. There had been a serious threat of invasion from Denmark, and it had been necessary to bring over a large army of Normans and Bretons to strengthen the existing army. Equipping and maintaining this new force had cost a lot of money. The Anglo-Saxon kings had financed their armies by means of a tax, the geld. (The infamous Danegeld was a precursor of this system – money had been collected to pay off the threat of Danish invasions in the 9th and 10th centuries.) It was obvious, by the end of 1085, that a further tax would have to be levied to replenish the royal treasury. It is possible that the royal government was also thinking of revising the way in which the tax was assessed. Perhaps, too, the threat of the Danish invasion in 1085 had raised in William's mind the question of the security of his rule. In the face of another invasion, could all the major landowners be relied upon to support him? Who was in control of the countryside 'on the ground'?

Unfortunately, the *Anglo-Saxon Chronicle* does not record King William's reasons, directly stated, for the decision to compile Domesday Book. This omission has led to one of the longest-running controversies in English history-writing. One group of historians has described Domesday Book as a tax book, a survey designed to up-date the royal administration's knowledge of the taxable value of the kingdom. The other major group of historians has seen Domesday Book as a feudal register, designed to sort out and record the details of landholding twenty years after the Conqueror had first started to grant out the lands of deposed Anglo-Saxon nobles to his Norman followers in return for their political and military support. Domesday Book, they argue, records not only who held what land directly from the king, and what services he had to render to the king in return, but also the land holdings and obligations of everyone else who occupied land, down to the poorest cottager. In addition, by so doing, the Norman government legitimised, retrospectively, the Conquest and the subsequent large-scale transfer of land by providing a register of title in which each lord's estate, and his title to that estate, were clearly recorded.

The booklist on p. 43 gives the titles of the most important books which outline both these lines of thought. These views are not totally incompatible, of course, and, whichever proves eventually to be the more correct, Domesday Book itself still survives as an invaluable record for the present-day reader to study and enjoy.

How Domesday Book was Made

We are not completely certain how Domesday Book was compiled, although recent research has done much to clarify the picture. The most helpful contemporary description of the way in which the information for Domesday Book was collected comes from the *Inquisitio Eliensis* (the Ely Inquest), one of the smaller, earlier surveys associated with Domesday Book. It recounts how royal commissioners were sent to each village where they met a jury of local men with detailed local knowledge who provided answers to the following questions:

what was the name of the manor?
who held it in the time of King Edward?
who holds it now?
how many hides are there?
how many ploughs in demesne? (on the home farm)
and how many belonging to the men?
how many villeins?
how many cottars?
how many slaves?
how many freemen?
how many sokemen?
how much woodland?
how much meadow?
how much pasture?
how many mills?
how many fisheries?
how much has been added to, or taken away from, the estate?
what did it use to be worth altogether?
what is it worth now?
how much does each freeman and sokeman have?

All this to be recorded three times: in the time of King Edward,
as it was when King William granted the estate, as it is now.
(To see how these questions were answered, turn to the sample Domesday entry on pp. 14–15)

A contemporary observer, Robert, Bishop of Hereford, writing shortly after Domesday Book was compiled, added that a second group of investigators, who had no personal connections with the areas they were responsible for, were given the task of checking the information gathered by the first group of commissioners.

Modern research has revealed further details of how Domesday Book was compiled. During the first stages of the investigation, information was put together by royal clerks in the king's treasury at Winchester, probably from pre-existing documents relating to earlier royal tax collections, and from written and verbal local evidence supplied by lords of manors themselves. One letter, from an important clergyman, discussing this stage of the procedure, has survived, providing an important clue for historians. Inquiries were also made by groups of commissioners in the localities.

Then the country seems to have been divided into eight administrative regions, called circuits, and the second group of commissioners, as described by Robert of Hereford, then visited the circuit to which they had been appointed to check that the information collected so far was correct. These commissioners were important and influential nobles, and it seems likely that they also had powers to settle any disputes which had arisen over rights to land. They held their inquiries at specially-convened meetings of the shire court, where important men in each county met to settle local disputes.

Once this process of checking was completed, a detailed record of the findings was drawn up, county by county, and the information was arranged, within each county, under the names of each lord of the manor. (It is not quite clear whether the information collected during the earliest stages of the Domesday inquiry was collected on a village-by-village basis, or organised from the start under the names of manorial lords.) These revised records were sent back to the royal clerks at Winchester, where, with the exception of Circuit 8, which described the eastern counties of Essex, Norfolk and Suffolk, they were standardised and abbreviated by highly-skilled royal scribes into the one volume of Great Domesday. The information relating to the eastern counties seems not to have been incorporated into the Great Domesday volume. It survives today as Little Domesday. It is less carefully-written and contains rather more detailed information than the Great Domesday volumes. It is taken to represent the sole surviving example of the commissioners' reports from which Great Domesday was compiled. Present-day users of Domesday Book will find that the quality of the text describing their town or village will depend on which volume it is in.

Historians have attempted to reconstruct all these detailed stages in the compilation of Domesday Book, incorporating a number of other contemporary surveys into their picture. This view of the way in which Domesday Book was compiled has several implications:
It explains why Domesday Book is in two volumes, and why they differ from each other. It also suggests that a large number of the documents which went towards the compilation of Domesday Book must have disappeared over the centuries, and, incidentally, reminds us of our good fortune in that Domesday Book itself has survived intact for 900 years. It also stands as a memorial to the skill and efficiency of the commissioners and clerks in the royal administration, who completed so huge and complicated a task in little more than eighteen months, before King William's death in September 1087.

The Domesday Text

The Contents of Domesday Book

The text of Domesday describes a large part of England, but with several major exceptions. Areas in the far North, which had only recently been pacified, or were not yet totally under Norman rule, are not covered by the survey; that is to say Northumberland, Durham, Cumberland and northern Westmorland, as well as Scotland and Wales. Among the towns, no information is given for London, Bristol or Winchester, to name the three most important omissions.

Within Domesday, information is arranged county by county. The map opposite shows the pattern of pre-1974 English counties. Domesday county boundaries followed approximately the same pattern, with the exception of Rutland and its neighbours. If in doubt as to the location of your town or village in relation to the Domesday pattern, see Darby's *Domesday Gazetteer* (see p. 43) for Domesday place names and county references.

Within each county, information is arranged under the names of the major landholders, not on a settlement by settlement basis. If the king holds lands in a county, then his name will head the list, and will be followed by the names of other important tenants-in-chief (who held their estates directly from the king) in approximate order of rank or local influence. Since more than one tenant-in-chief could, and did, hold lands within the boundaries of each settlement, it can be a difficult task to make sure that you have located all the Domesday entries for your own town or village. The indexes to the Phillimore volumes (see p. 13) can be a great help here. In addition, some minor tenants are referred to only by their first names, and possibilities for confusion of identity can arise. Again, reference can be made to the Phillimore name indexes.

Furthermore, not all present-day settlements are mentioned in Domesday. A few are post-1086 developments, for example, King's Lynn, which grew up as a trading post on the shores of the Wash in the 12th century. Other settlements are sometimes 'lost' in the Domesday record as part of a larger, neighbouring, unit, or aggregated into a greater whole, as seems to have been the case for the small, scattered farmsteads of the West Country uplands.

The Counties of Domesday Book

1	Cumberland	28	Suffolk
2	Northumberland	29	Wiltshire
3	Westmoreland	30	Berkshire
4	Durham	31	Oxfordshire
5	Lancashire	32	Hertfordshire
6	Yorkshire	33	Essex
7	Cheshire	34	Middlesex
8	Derbyshire	35	Surrey
9	Nottinghamshire	36	Hampshire
10	Lincolnshire	37	Somerset
11	Flintshire	38	Dorset
12	Shropshire	39	Devon
13	Staffordshire	40	Cornwall
14	Leicestershire	41	Kent
15	Rutland	42	Sussex
16	Herefordshire		
17	Worcestershire		Wales (not in Domesday Book)
18	Warwickshire	43	Carnarvon
19	Northamptonshire	44	Denbigh
20	Huntingdonshire	45	Merioneth
21	Cambridgeshire	46	Montgomery
22	Norfolk	47	Cardigan
23	Monmouthshire	48	Radnor
24	Gloucestershire	49	Pembroke
25	Oxfordshire	50	Carmarthen
26	Buckinghamshire	51	Brecknock
27	Bedfordshire	52	Glamorgan

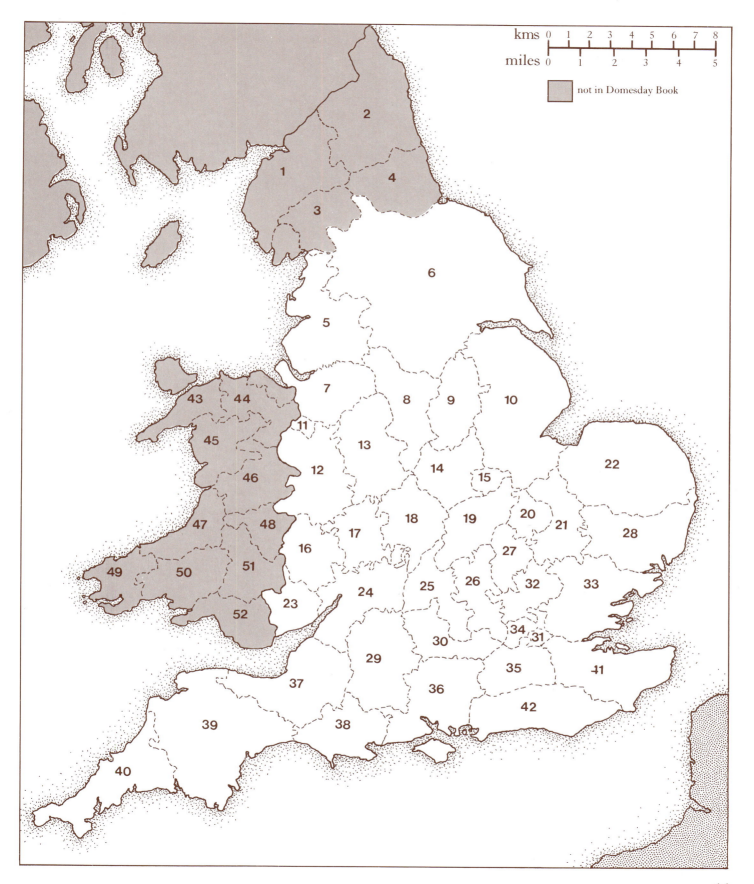

kms 0 1 2 3 4 5 6 7 8

miles 0 1 2 3 4 5

not in Domesday Book

11

Domesday Population

Domesday mentions about 275,000 people in its pages. Since the compilers were interested in the value of the land, and who held it, rather than the total population, this figure refers to heads of households only, not complete families. It is therefore necessary to multiply the Domesday figure by a number chosen to represent the size of the average eleventh-century household. This will convert it into a rough total population of the areas covered by Domesday Book.

We do not know the size of the average household at the time of Domesday. All we can do is to use the figure, called a 'multiplier', worked out by historians who have studied the population of later centuries. They have records of Baptisms, Marriages and Burials to work from. They have found, for the sixteenth and seventeenth centuries, when the records start, that the average size of household was around five. That is, mother, father, and three surviving children, though more children may have been born and have died in infancy. There might also be living-in servants.

If the Domesday figure of 275,000 people is multiplied by five, it gives a total population of around 1½ million. The sample entry of Wymondham has a population of about 1620 (=324×5). Population was more densely-settled in the southern and eastern counties, as it is today. The land there was more fertile, and the climate milder. There had also been an influx of Scandinavian settlers in the previous centuries.

Domesday Book in Print

The Domesday text was first published in two volumes by the Record Commissioners in 1783, in a typeface known as 'record type' which attempted to reproduce all the abbreviations and 'shorthand' signs of the original. A photozincograph facsimile of the original manuscript was issued by the Ordnance Survey in county volumes between 1861–64. Since 1900, translations of the Domesday text, with scholarly introductions, have been published in the county volumes of the Victoria History of the Counties of England. Volumes for the whole country have not yet been published, although work is in progress towards completing the series. A list of volumes already published will be found opposite.

1986 should see the completion of the most recent attempt to publish the Domesday text in translation. This series, published by Phillimore, contains a reduced facsimile of the 1783 text with a modern translation on facing pages. Each volume also contains notes, indices of place and personal names, and a glossary. A list is given opposite. Many scholars have expressed reservations about some of the terms used in the translations – for example, 'villanus', one type of manorial tenant, is rendered as 'villager'. This is not incorrect, but does rather beg a large number of very complex questions about the status of Domesday tenants. In spite of these criticisms, the series as a whole represents a tremendously useful resource for the local historian.

Domesday Society

king → * tenant in chief → sub-tenant → freemen / sokemen / townsmen (burgess)

king → * tenant in chief → villein / bordar / cottar / slave

* lords of the manor

Volumes in the Victoria History of the Counties of England series with Domesday text

County	Vol. No.	Editor	Date of Publication
Bedfordshire	I	H.A. Doubleday & W. Page	1905
Berkshire	I	P.H. Ditchfield & W. Page	1906
Buckinghamshire	I	W. Page	1905
Cambridgeshire	I	L.F. Salzman	1938
Cornwall	II pt. 8	W. Page	1924
Cumberland	I	not named	1901
Derbyshire	I	W. Page	1905
Devonshire	I	W. Page	1906
Dorset	III	R.B. Pugh	1968
Essex	I	not named	1903
Hampshire	I	H.A. Doubleday & W. Page	1900
Herefordshire	I	W. Page	1908
Huntingdonshire	I	W. Page & G. Proby	1926
Kent	III	W. Page	1932
Lancashire	I	W. Farrer & J. Brownbill	1906
Leicestershire	I	W. Page	1907
Middlesex	I	J.S. Cockburn, H.P.F. King & K.G.T. McDonnell	1969
Norfolk	II	W. Page	1906
Northamptonshire	I	W.R.D. Adkins & R.M. Serjeantson	1902
Nottinghamshire	I	W. Page	1906
Oxfordshire	I	L.F. Salzman	1939
Rutland	I	W. Page	1908
Shropshire	I	W. Page	1908
Somerset	II	W. Page	1911
Staffordshire	IV	L.M. Midgley	1958
Suffolk	I	W. Page	1911
Surrey	I	H.E. Malden	1902
Sussex	I	W. Page	1905
Warwickshire	I	H.A. Doubleday & W. Page	1904
Wiltshire	II	R.B. Pugh & E. Crittal	1955
Worcestershire	I	J.W. Willis-Bund & H.A. Doubleday	1901
Yorkshire	II	W. Page	1912

Volumes in the Phillimore translations of Domesday Book

Vol. No.	County	Date of Publication
1	Kent	1983
2	Sussex	1976
3	Surrey	1975
4	Hampshire	1982
5	Berkshire	1979
6	Wiltshire	1979
7	Dorset	1983
8	Somerset	1980
9	Devon (2 vols)	1985
10	Cornwall	1979
11	Middlesex	1975
12	Hertfordshire	1976
13	Buckinghamshire	1978
14	Oxfordshire	1978
15	Gloucestershire	1982
16	Worcestershire	1982
17	Herefordshire	1983
18	Cambridgeshire	1981
19	Huntingdonshire	1975
20	Bedfordshire	1977
21	Northamptonshire	1979
22	Leicestershire	1979
23	Warwickshire	1976
24	Staffordshire	1976
25	Shropshire	1985
26	Cheshire	1978
27	Derbyshire	1978
28	Nottinghamshire	1977
29	Rutland	1980
30	Yorkshire	1985
31	Lincolnshire and claims in Yorks.	1985
32	Essex	1983
33	Norfolk (2 vols)	1984
34	Suffolk (2 vols)	1985

Sample Text of one Domesday Manor

Translation of Sample Entry

Line 1: Forehoe hundred: Stigand held Wymondham in the time of King Edward.

Line 2: 4 carucates of land. Always 60 villeins and 50 bordars and 8 slaves. Always

Line 3: 4 ploughs on the demesne. Then 60 ploughs belonging to the men, now 24; Ralph Wader made this

Line 4: confusion (disturbance) before he forefeited (his lands), and they

Line 5: could all be restored. Then woodland (for) 100 pigs, now for 60. 60 acres meadow.

Line 6: Always 2 mills and 1 fishery. Always two rounceys (riding horses) 16 cattle, and 50 pigs

Line 7: and 24 sheep. 87 sokemen were attached to this manor in the time of King Edward,

Line 8: now only 18, and they have 30 acres of land. Always

Line 9: 1 plough. There is a further sokeman with one carucate of land. Always 4 villeins and

Line 10: 10 bordars and one mill and wood for 16 pigs and 4 acres meadow.

Line 11: This manor with all soke (rights of jurisdiction) was worth with soke £20

Line 12: now (£) 60, and it is 2 leagues long and 1 league wide,

Line 13: and pays geld of 6s 8d. Among those sokemen who have been taken away,

Line 14: William de Warenne has 55. And they have under them 57 bordars.

Line 15: Between them all they have 5 carucates of land and 12 acres of meadow and in the time of King Edward they had 20

Line 16: ploughs, now 13 and half a mill. Always valued at £10. And Ralph

Line 17: de Bellafago has 10 sokemen, 2 carucates of land and 32 bordars.

Line 18: Always 7 ploughs and 12 acres of meadow and 1½ mills. And Count

Line 19: Alan (has) one sokeman, 1½ carucates of land and 13 bordars and 3 ploughs and

Line 20: 9 acres of meadow and 1 mill and the value is 30s. And Roger Bigot (has)

Line 21: 2 sokemen and 45 acres land and 6 bordars and 2 ploughs and 2 acres

Line 22: of meadow. Woodland (for) 60 pigs, now 16. Value 7s 6d.

Line 1: Færhou Ħ. Wimundhā tenuit Stigand tépr · r · e ·

Line 2: iiii · car tre · Semp · lx · uill · & l · bord · 7 viii · ser · semp

Line 3: iii · car indnio · tño lx car hom · m xxiiii · hanc con

Line 4: fusione fcd hadt de wapt anteq foris facerit · & omis pot

Line 5: sent restaurari · Tñc silua · c · por · m · lx · 7 lx · ac ptu

Line 6: semp · ii · mol · & i · pisc · semp · ii · r · 7 xvi · añ · 7 l · por ·

Line 7: & xx · iiii · ou · huic manerio iacebant · t · r · e · lxxx

Line 8: vii soc · m tantum xviii · hdt · xxx · ac tre · semp

Line 9: i · car · & adhuc · i · soc · i · car tre · semp · iiii · uill · 7

Line 10: x bord · & i · mol · silua xvi porc · & iiii · ac ptu ·

Line 11: hoc maneriu cu tota soca ualebat · t · r · e · e soca xx ·

Line 12: lib · m · lx · & hdt · ii · leug inlong · 7 i · in lat · 7 vi · sol ·

Line 13: 7 viii · d de gelto · Ex his sokemanis qui abbati sñt

Line 14: hdt Wills de uuar · lv · 7 hdt subse · lvii · bord · intcotu

Line 15: hdt · v · car tre · & xii · ac ptu · 7 tépr · r · e · habebant · xx ·

Line 16: car · m · xiii · & dim mol · semp ual x · lib · & Radulf

Line 17: de bellafago · habet · x · soc · ii · car tre · 7 xxx ii · bor ·

Line 18: semp · vii · car · 7 xii · ac ptu · 7 i · mol · 7 dim · & comes

Line 19: alan · i · soc · i · car tre · 7 dim · 7 xiii · bord · 7 iii · car 7

Line 20: ix ac ptu & i · mol · 7 ual xxx · sol · ∫ & Rog bigot

Line 21: ii soc · xl · v · ac tre · 7 vi · bord · 7 ii car · 7 ii · ac

Line 22: ptu tño silua ix por · m · xvi · 7 ual vii · sol · 7 vi · d ·

∫ Blawefelle Ħ · Torp ten stigand archiepc ·

t · r · e · iii · car tre · tñc xx iiii · uill · p xx iii · m xxii ·

Summary Diagram of Sample Domesday Text

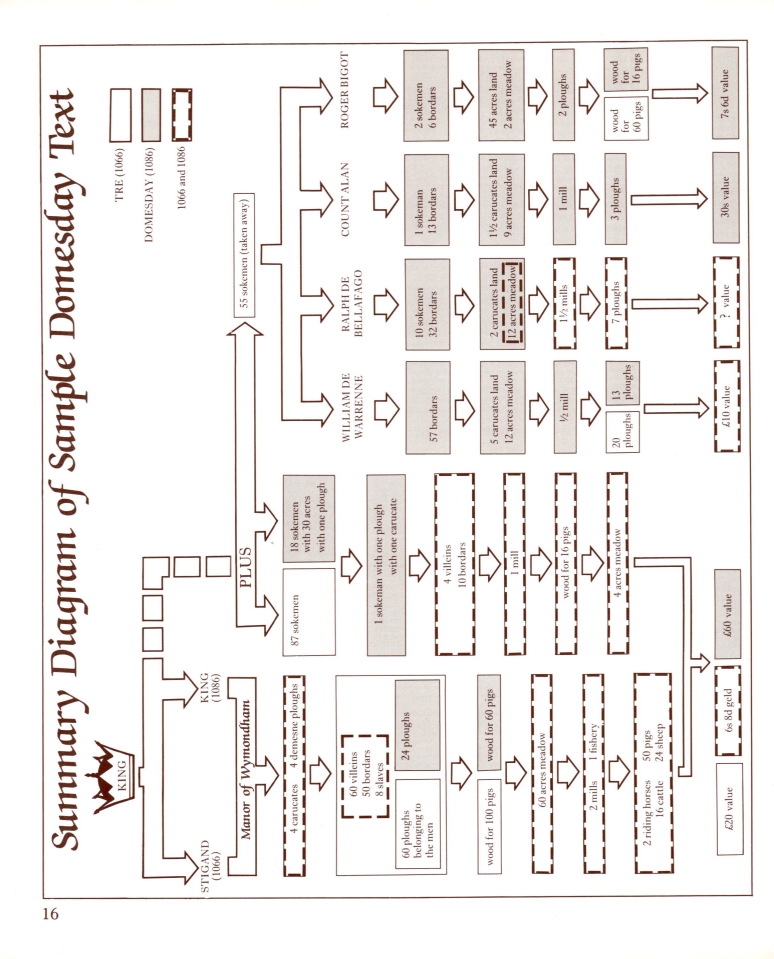

Legend:
- TRE (1066)
- DOMESDAY (1086)
- 1066 and 1086

KING

STIGAND (1066) → KING (1086)

Manor of Wymondham

4 carucates → 4 demesne ploughs →

- 60 villeins / 50 bordars / 8 slaves
- 24 ploughs
- 60 ploughs belonging to the men

→ wood for 60 pigs / wood for 100 pigs → 60 acres meadow → 2 mills / 1 fishery → 2 riding horses / 16 cattle / 50 pigs / 24 sheep →

£60 value / 6s 8d geld / £20 value

PLUS

- 18 sokemen with 30 acres with one plough
- 87 sokemen

→ 1 sokeman with one plough with one carucate → 4 villeins / 10 bordars → 1 mill → wood for 16 pigs → 4 acres meadow →

55 sokemen (taken away) →

WILLIAM DE WARRENNE
- 57 bordars → 5 carucates land / 12 acres meadow → ½ mill → 20 ploughs / 13 ploughs → £10 value

RALPH DE BELLAFAGO
- 10 sokemen / 32 bordars → 2 carucates land / 12 acres meadow → 1½ mills → 7 ploughs → ? value

COUNT ALAN
- 1 sokeman / 13 bordars → 1½ carucates land / 9 acres meadow → 1 mill → 3 ploughs → 30s value

ROGER BIGOT
- 2 sokemen / 6 bordars → 45 acres land / 2 acres meadow → 2 ploughs → wood for 16 pigs / wood for 60 pigs → 7s 6d value

Did Wealth equal Freedom?
Personal Status and Land-holding in Domesday Book

Various terms are used to describe the manorial tenants in Domesday Book. Some occur throughout England, others have a strictly local distribution. Some terms are used to describe personal status, that is, a person's freedom or otherwise from manorial burdens in the form of rents or labour services, and their freedom to leave their lord's lands. Other terms are used to describe the types of tenure by which land is held. Yet others refer to the amount of land an individual holds. It is important to remember that, in Domesday Book, wealth and freedom from manorial burdens do not always coincide. A man may be the tenant of a fairly large holding, and yet owe his lord heavy services in return for his land. In contrast, a poor cottager with only a house and garden plot may owe very light labour services to his lord in return for his holding. In one sense, the wealthy tenant is 'better off'; in another sense the poor cottager is more 'free'.

The following list attempts, therefore, to clarify a position which was by no means simple even at the time of Domesday, and which grew in complexity throughout the Middle Ages. The various groups of tenants are described in descending order of freedom from manorial control.

Tenant in chief: a 'lord of the manor'; held his estate directly from the king, in return for military service and/or political support. In Domesday Book, he is usually a Norman lord, loyal to William the Conqueror, who has replaced a dispossessed Anglo-Saxon. Some great lords 'sub-let' parts of their estates to lesser lords. These became the lords of the manors they held in all practical respects.

Freemen: the highest-ranking group of tenants mentioned in Domesday. They held land in return for rents and/or services, like other tenants, but were free to leave their land or 'go with it' to seek the political protection of another lord. Sometimes, they were required to ask their lord's permission to do this. They were obliged to attend the manorial court held by their lord for his tenants, and also whichever soke or hundred court had acquired jurisdiction over them.

Sokemen: the next highest-ranking tenant in Domesday. It is often difficult to see why a distinction is made between freemen and sokemen, since they seem to hold land on very similar terms. There is, however, some uncertainty about how free all sokemen were to leave their lands, or 'go with them' to another lord.

Villein: the archetypal manorial tenant, holding land in return for performing labour services on the lord's demesne, and rendering other rents in money and/or in kind. They were bound to the lord's land, and could not leave it without the lord's permission and the payment of a fine. Villeins could hold quite substantial amounts of land. Although bound to the land, they were personally free, at least in the Anglo-Saxon law relating to murder fines which defined a man's worth in the eyes of society.

Bordar: a manorial tenant of lower status in the village community than a villein, typically holding a smaller amount of land from the lord. Like the villein, bound to the lord's land but accorded the dignity of a free man by Anglo-Saxon murder-fine law.

Cottar: the poorest class of manorial tenants, typically holding a cottage and garden, with only a little agricultural land. Bound to the lord's land, but still free when contrasted with a slave.

Slave: a survival from pre-Conquest times. There were a fair number of slaves in Anglo-Saxon society. They held no land (or not for longer than their lifetime) and were the property of their lords, in that they could be brought and sold. Slavery was also used as a punishment, and a destitute individual could even sell himself or his children into slavery. It was the lord's duty to feed, clothe and house his slaves. Although they are mentioned in Domesday, slaves gradually disappeared from English society in the century after the Conquest.

There is a reasonable amount of evidence to suggest that the position of the lower and/or poorer groups of tenants was worsening between 1066–1086. If slavery was disappearing, the ties which bound a poor free bordar or cottar to his lord were strengthening. Villeins and below were being denied access to the royal courts, one of the hallmarks of a free man, and the practical power of the lord, as the ultimate 'owner' (after the king) of all the land, to whom rents and services must be paid, was increasing.

Domesday Book Terminology

Domesday Book was compiled from written returns and verbal testimony in which a wide variety of local terms relating to local agricultural conditions and social customs were used. Most of these terms were of Anglo-Saxon or Danish origin, and were expressed in Old English. The compilers of Domesday Book translated many of these into Latin, thereby adding the possibility of linguistic confusion to an already complicated picture. As the Anglo-Saxon Chronicle reports (see p. 36), the commissioners were working to a closely-defined brief. But, while attempting to standardise, they also took care to try and render accurately the fine distinctions in status or tenure which would have been so clear, and so important, to the villagers who gave evidence to the Domesday enquiry. The present-day historian, in trying to reconstruct conditions 'on the ground' from the sometimes enigmatic Domesday entries, is faced with the commissioners' problem in reverse. Nowhere are Domesday terms defined in general; we can only work out the meaning of words such as 'sokeman' or 'villein' by reference to the contexts in which they occur, and by consulting the work of historians who have made an intensive study of this topic. The following glossary is intended to serve as a general guide, and lists only the most frequently-used terms. For a guide to particular 'problem' words in a local context, see the introductions to the Victoria County History translations of the Domesday text, and the notes to the Phillimore county volumes. The best guide to the meaning of basic Domesday terminology is still Maitland, *Domesday Book and Beyond*, (see booklist p. 43).

Domesday Glossary

Acre: unit of land measurement, variable in size. Used in Domesday to indicate the amount of land that could be ploughed in a day.

Barton: outlying farm, usually for corn; often associated with ecclesiastical estates.

Berewick: outlying settlement, part of a manor.

Bordar: manorial tenant of relatively low status, usually with a small holding of land.

Boor (*gebur*): manorial tenant of fairly low status, sometimes identified with *colibertus*, a freed man.

Bovate: unit of land measure; one-eighth of a *carucate*.

Carucate: unit of land measurement, roughly equivalent to a *hide*, used in the former *Danelaw*. Often taken to equal approximately 120 acres. Recent research has suggested that Domesday carucates may also represent a revised system of taxation.

Colibertus: a manorial tenant, a freedman (i.e. formerly a slave), perhaps with land and a plough. Often used to translate Old English 'gebur'.

Cottar: a manorial tenant of low status, a cottager, usually without much land.

Danelaw: the lands formerly under the control of the Danes; in Domesday, East Yorkshire, Nottinghamshire, Lincolnshire, Norfolk and Suffolk.

Demesne: the 'home farm' of the lord of the manor; his own estate, cultivated for him either by his manorial tenants as part of the rents and services they owed him, or by hired labourers and servants. Sometimes rented out, or 'farmed', for a money payment.

Farmer: someone who undertakes to run an estate or some other profitable enterprise for its proprietor in return for making a regular money payment to them.

Fee: a lord's holding, often originally granted to him in return for the performance of specific services.

Firma ('farm'): a fixed sum paid to the king or to a lord in place of services or other payments (sometimes in kind) owing to them.

Freeman: a manorial tenant who held his land free of any labour services owing to his lord.

Furlong: a unit of land measurement; originally one-twelfth of a league.

Geld: the principal royal tax in the 10th and 11th centuries; originally collected to pay off the Danish invaders. Believed by Round to have been levied at the time of Domesday according to an assessment based on hides, but recent research has suggested that Domesday geld was levied on the total value of each manor.

Hide: a ploughland, a unit of land measurement, often taken to equal approximately 120 acres. Also a unit of taxation. Wide variations in area between hides can be found throughout Domesday; also, hides 'on the ground' and 'taxation' hides do not always correlate.

Hundred: a subdivision of a shire. It held a court which met approximately once a month to deal with petty 'police' cases, and which was attended by representatives from the hundred's component villages and other important local figures.

Lathe: (found in Kent) a subdivision of a shire containing several hundreds.

League: a measure of length; approximately 1½ miles.

Leet: (found in East Anglia) subdivision of a hundred, containing one large village or several smaller ones. It held a court, which met once or twice a year, and, like the hundred courts, dealt with petty 'police' cases. Many leet courts were taken over by manorial lords and administered by them. The leet system is thought by some authorities to pre-date the division of shires into hundreds.

Manor: an estate with dependent tenants (of various degrees of freedom) and often including rights of jurisdiction over them. Held by a lord of the manor from a superior lord or directly from the king. Often defined in Domesday in relation to the payment of geld.

Mark: a unit of currency; if silver, worth 13s 4d; if gold, worth £6.

Ora: a unit of currency of Danish origin; worth either 16d or 12d.

Perch: a unit of land measurement; usually 16½ feet.

Reeve: a royal officer. Sheriff = shire-reeve.

Radman: radknight: a manorial tenant, a freeman of relatively high status. He originally served his lord as an escort, or by riding with messages.

Rent: a payment made, usually to a superior, in return for lands held. Some rents were paid in money, others in kind.

Sake: jurisdiction exercised by a lord over his tenants or other men.

Soke: another kind of jurisdiction exercised by lords, which included the right to receive fines and other payments from those convicted. Also used to indicate the area over which this right was exercised.

Sokeman: a man liable to attend the court of particular soke, and/or liable to perform certain relatively light duties for his lord in return for lands held in 'socage' tenure. One of the highest-status tenants, after freemen, in Domesday.

Sulung: found in Kent, a unit of land measurement, approximately 200 acres.

Sester: a dry measure, of variable size, perhaps 32 oz.

T.R.E.: *Tempore Regis Edwardi*, in the time of King Edward (the Confessor), i.e. 1066. One of the points at which the Domesday commissioners were asked to evaluate the lands they surveyed.

Thane: an Anglo-Saxon term for a minor nobleman, formerly used to describe the king's military companions and, later, his ministers. In Domesday used to refer to a man holding land from the king by special grant.

Vill: settlement; a translation of the Anglo-Saxon 'tun' which could refer to both villages and small towns.

Villein: a manorial tenant, of intermediate status, with a substantial holding of land. He performed labour services on his lord's estate.

Sample Interpretation – what Domesday tells us

The following 'worked example' is put forward as one possible model for interpreting the Domesday text. Many teachers may not wish to examine the text in such detail. It is suggested that they turn straight to the Summary diagram on p. 16. Further information about some of the terms used in Domesday can be found in the Glossary on pp. 18–19, and in the note on Personal Status and Land-holding on p. 17.

The extract on p. 14 is taken from Volume II of the Domesday survey, known as Little Domesday. (The Great Domesday volume contains rather less information about livestock than Little Domesday, and the precise amount of information given for each village will vary.) It describes the village of Wymondham in Norfolk, which lies about 10 miles south of Norwich. The place name, 'Wymondham' = 'Wigmund's ham (village)', suggests that this was a Saxon settlement and therefore already several centuries old in 1086. Certainly, by the time of Domesday Book, it was one of the largest villages in Norfolk measured in terms of population, although this population was spread fairly thinly over a wide area. We can work out this distribution because, unusually for East Anglia, the parish boundary of Wymondham encircles approximately the same area as the pre-Conquest manor, whose dimensions are given in lines 12/13 of the Domesday text, once allowance has been made for woods and common lands between neighbouring villages. (A league is approximately 1½ miles.) It is more usual to find several manors within the boundary of one settlement in this part of the country. To make sure that you have traced all the entries in Domesday relating to your town or village, check the Phillimore place indexes (see pp. 12–13).

The Domesday entry for Wymondham tells us that it was in the king's hands in 1086 – it is listed under the heading 'the king holds'. It also tells us that Stigand held the manor in the time of King Edward, i.e. in 1066. Stigand was Archbishop of Canterbury at the time of the Conquest, and one of the most important men in the kingdom. (The introductions to the *Victoria County History* volumes, and the Phillimore name indexes will give you information about the Domesday and pre-Conquest landholders; see pp. 12–13.)

Line 2 tells us that Stigand's home farm, or demesne, contained 4 carucates of land: approximately 480 acres of arable. He had 60 villeins and 50 bordars bound to work for him on this estate. Presumably they held additional land of their own, since they had 60 ploughs in 1066 between them with which to work it (line 3). There were 4 ploughs on Stigand's demesne farm; a neat equation with the number of carucates or ploughlands. In both instances, 'ploughs' implies also the animals to pull the plough. Usually up to 8 oxen were needed. Occasionally horses were used. In line 4 we learn that the tenants' ploughs have been reduced to 24, though they could be restored. This information presumably relates to the unsuccessful rising against the Norman conquerors which took place in East Anglia in 1075. Earl Ralph had been one of the ringleaders, and presumably some of the tenants in Wymondham had followed him in the rising. Ralph was deprived of his estates, and there may have been reprisals against the other participants. Contemporaries commented on the Normans' ferocity during the 'harrying of the North', when large areas of the countryside were laid waste after a rising led by a group of northern nobles.

As well as the villeins and bordars, who were bound to their plots of land and obliged to perform labour services on the lord of the manor's demesne, there were also 87 sokemen attached to the manor in Stigand's time. They were freer than the villeins and bordars but could not normally leave their manorial lord to seek the political protection of another lord, taking their land with them to enlarge their new lord's estates. However, a large number of the Wymondham sokemen seem to have done just this between 1066 and 1086, perhaps during the time of Earl Ralph's revolt, perhaps after Stigand had been replaced in office in 1078. We see (in line 14) that William de Warenne, a great Norman noble who held lands nearby, had drawn 55 of these sokemen into his orbit, and that (lines 16/17) Ralph de Bellafago had acquired 10. To a lesser degree, Count Alan and Roger Bigot have done the same (lines 19–21).

To turn to livestock, line 5 reveals that there is wood for 60 pigs, though there had previously been enough to provide forage for 100. In East Anglia, wood is always described in terms of its capacity to feed pigs, rather than by its area. This is not the case elsewhere. Maybe some of the trees had been cut down for building purposes? There are 60 acres of meadow. Presumably this lay along the banks of the two streams which flow through the village. Meadow, which provided hay for winter animal fodder, was a very valuable asset.

The mills mentioned in line 6 would have been water mills, also by the streams. The characteristic medieval post-mill which appears so charmingly in many manuscript illustrations did not reach England until the 12th century. Perhaps the fishery (line 6) was in one of the mill ponds? Fisheries were an important resource. They provided food for fast-days, and a source of fresh fish for inland settlements. References to salt or smoked fish are common in medieval writings. Quite how palatable or wholesome these were is doubtful!

Two riding-horses are mentioned (line 6). Horses were highly valued by the Norman nobility as one of the vital components of their military machine. The mounted Norman knights had wreaked havoc among the Saxon foot-soldiers at Hastings. Relatively few cattle (16), apart from the plough oxen, are kept (line 6) but it is worth noting that the woodland is stocked nearly to capacity with pigs. The sheep (line 7) would have grazed on the common lands (not mentioned in the survey, but implied, since no village could function without them) and probably on the stubble in the arable fields after harvest.

The 18 sokemen mentioned in lines 7/8 hold 30 acres of land between them, so it is unlikely that any of them had a substantial holding, even though we are not told how the land is divided up between them. They can be contrasted with the single sokeman mentioned in line 9, who seems to hold something rather like a sub-manor, with a whole carucate of land, dependent tenants beneath him (4 villeins, 10 bordars), and his own mill and meadowland, plus grazing rights for pigs (line 10). Maybe he was a settler in an outlying hamlet, or berewick, which had been brought under the control of Stigand's main manor sometime in the past.

In lines 11/12 we are told that the king, as Stigand's successor, has rights of jurisdiction, and profits of jurisdiction over all the manor's inhabitants. The whole manor was valued at £20 when first granted out to a Norman lord, and at £60 in 1086. We are not given its value in 1066. Geld (line 13), or tax, was assessed in East Anglia in the Domesday survey as an actual sum of money, rather than as a potential value based on *hidage*

(see glossary), which was the usual arrangement in other parts of the country. Wymondham was worth, in the eyes of the Domesday valuers, quite a substantial sum. Comparative geld values for neighbouring villages can give some indication of their relative importance. These figures may have to be assembled from information listed in Domesday Book under several different manors.

Four other lords are described (lines 14–20) as having lands in Wymondham. They are all mentioned in Domesday's list of tenants-in-chief, and all held land in neighbouring villages. The tenants in Wymondham over whom they have rights are not the usual range of manorial tenants; they have only sokemen and bordars under them. None of the lords is mentioned as having demesne.

Domesday Checklist

Questions to ask about the Domesday entry for your town or village:

* how many manors?
* which lord holds each manor?
* who held it formerly? what do we know about him?
* how big is the home farm (demesne)?
* what agricultural equipment is mentioned?
* what other resources (mills, fisheries etc)?
* what livestock is mentioned?
* how many freemen or sokemen?
* how many other tenants?
* how many slaves?
* how much land do the tenants hold?
* what equipment and livestock do they have?
* what other information is given about land use (woods, meadow, pasture etc)?
* are any other sorts of buildings named?
* is a value given for the land?
* what was it taxed at?
* is there any evidence of changes 1066–1086?
* is there any evidence of 'politics' e.g. revolt or resistance to the Normans?
* if your entry describes a town, what evidence of urban activities or special privileges is mentioned?

The Domesday Landscape

The drawing opposite is a very rough approximation of what the landscape of the village of Wymondham in Norfolk might have looked like in 1086. It is based on the Domesday entry on p. 14.

Domesday gives us several clues about the landscape. By 1086, many of the countryside's most important features were already fixed, or were becoming so. Churches (1), field boundaries (2), roads (3), and bridges (4) are likely to be among the most stable features of the landscape, although even these may change position quite radically over the centuries in certain localities.

The Domesday text often gives the size of the lord's demesne (5) and sometimes the size of the whole manor as well. It is worth comparing these dimensions with any information you can discover about the size of a lord's estate at a later date. This sort of information, and much else of use when reconstructing a landscape, is often included in published local histories of your area. Some volumes of the Victoria County Histories (see p. 13) have chapters on landscape and buildings; other useful general books are listed on pp. 43–44).

Ordnance Survey maps will also show the modern parish boundary (6). In many areas, this will not have changed substantially since 1086. If more than one lord held a manor in your village, a comparison of the different lords' entries might help to locate their estates 'on the ground'. Did they, for example, all have fisheries and watermills or meadowland, or equal amounts of woodlands?

Intelligent guesswork also has a part to play in reconstructing the Domesday landscape. You would expect to find meadowland (7) along the banks of any streams and rivers (8). Watermills (9) and fisheries (10) might be found close together; the millpond would provide calm, deep water for rearing fish.

Place name evidence can provide additional clues. The road leading to the watermill at Wymondham is called 'Damgate Street' (11).

Woodland (12) and common land (13) can sometimes be located through early maps; check what is available in your local County Record Office. Old maps may also show ancient common land between villages, and perhaps old field boundaries, too. All these maps will be at least 500 years later than Domesday book but many of them show the old open-field pattern of farming, itself developed from the Domesday arrangement of cultivation. Your local history library may also contain the reports of local groups who have worked on hedgerow-counting, that is, estimating the age of boundary hedges by counting the number of species. Woodland could be either 'wild' or planted.

Archaeologists have excavated various Anglo-Saxon sites, and we therefore have a reasonably accurate picture of what Domesday housing might have been like. We do not know what proportion of Wymondham's population lived in the village centre or how many lived in outlying settlements. It is tempting to guess that the villeins and bordars of the lord's manor were clustered together in the village centre, and the freemen and sokemen had settled in the outlying hamlets. Place name evidence suggests that there were four small settlements within the parish boundary. The writings of local historians, and the study of Ordnance Survey maps, will tell you whether your region is one where small, scattered hamlets or large, centralised villages predominated.

The site of the lord's manor house at the time of Domesday is likely to have been near the church, and probably near the centre of the village. Even though the house itself will not have survived, the name 'manor house' applied to a later building may give a clue to the site of an earlier building, although it is not possible to be certain from Domesday evidence alone.

Landscape Checklist

Look for the following clues about the Domesday landscape:

* parish boundaries
* churches
* roads
* rivers and bridges
* field boundaries and hedges
* earthworks, especially moated sites
* place names
* soil types and drainage
* local settlement patterns
* field names ⎫
* woodland ⎬ especially in conjunction with old maps
* common land ⎭

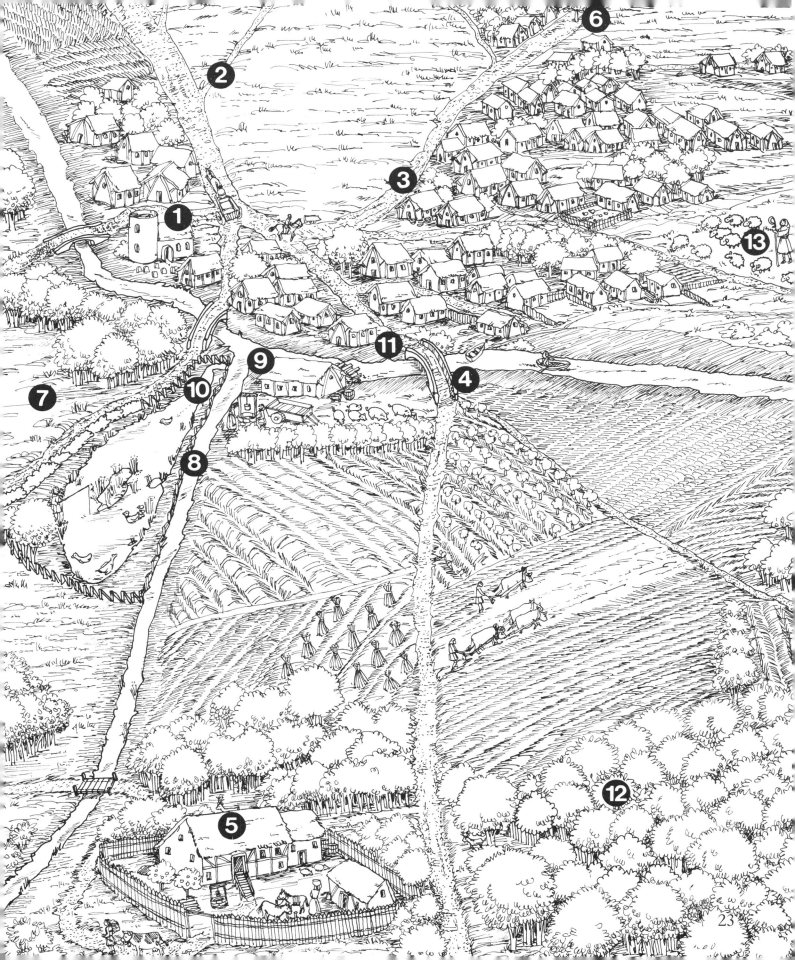

23

Domesday Projects:

Things to Do

The following projects are offered as suggestions for individual or class work based on Domesday Book. The project pages may be photocopied if desired for children to use on their own. Two versions are given of the 'Make a Seal' and 'Make a Quill Pen' projects. One version needs adult supervision, the alternative versions are safe for children to undertake by themselves. The 'Domesday Drama' project page is for teachers to use, rather than children. Answers to the puzzle pages are given on p.48.

The projects suggested on the following pages are only some of the many that could be based on Domesday Book. Other possibilities include:

* 'junk' models of the Domesday landscape, with people, animals, buildings etc.

* models of Domesday agricultural equipment, for example ploughs or watermills. Use manuscript pictures (see list on p. 44) for reference.

* a 'Domesday' account of the school, using survey techniques to describe the size of the school and the classes; the amount of land it occupies; other resources, such as a playground, garden, pool, sports field etc; also 'livestock' (pets), staff, and helpers. A 'then and now' element could be incorporated by investigating the recent history of the school. What was it like twenty years ago? Can former pupils be interviewed, or old photographs and plans be studied?

* models of Anglo-Saxon houses or Norman motte-and-bailey castles. You could also make various banners, of the sort that lords would have displayed in the great halls of their later stone-built castles.

Wordsquare Puzzle

```
S Q M E A D O W W W O O D J
T V R P D E M E S N E F E O
M I L L O K A B W P E R F X
A L O Z M A N O R A O E I E
P L R S E M O R E S P E S N
G E L D S Q R D D T L M H Z
A I (H I D E) T A W U O A E P
B N S L A V E R E R U N R L
M Z I S Y C A R E G M Y O
C O T T A R B F D T H F J U
T N S O K E M A N B A E L G
W I L L I A M H A R O L D H
```

This wordsquare contains 16 hidden words connected with Domesday Book. Search for the words by reading across and down the square. Two words occur twice within the puzzle. When you have found the words, circle them on the wordsquare, and tick them off on the list of clues. One has been done already for you. The answers are given on p. 48.

CLUES TO WORDSQUARE

* tenant of manor
* grass grown for hay
* lots of trees
* lord's home farm
* grinds corn
* tax
* the book of 1086
* estate with tenants
* area for tax collecting ✓
* man owned by another

* the amount of land that
    could be ploughed in a day
* man with a cottage and a little land
* where animals graze
* tool used to prepare land before sowing corn
* not a slave
* the conqueror
* King defeated at Hastings
* this man sounds as if he's got rather wet!

Project: Make a Seal

At the time of Domesday Book, most people could not read and write. Even great lords and ladies relied on specially-trained scribes and clerks to read and write letters and other documents for them. Because they could not sign their names, or recognise anyone else's signature, important people used seals to show that a document was genuine and not a forgery.

These seals were made of a small blob of wax, marked with the lord's own private sign. These signs were like little pictures; sometimes they showed a warrior on horseback, or a shield, or a castle. Anyone who received a letter with a seal would be able to recognise the picture on it. Then they would know that the letter was genuine.

Some seals from the time of Domesday book, or a little later, can still be seen today in museums. You can make a seal with your own special design on it, and learn how to fasten it on to a document as they would have done in Domesday times.

You will need:
plaster of Paris and water
Plasticine
petroleum jelly
thin cardboard
sticky tape
paper and pencil
scissors
blunt knife **or**
a special tool for modelling Plasticine
sealing wax
matches
plus an adult to help you with them

1 Draw the picture you would like on your seal. Keep it simple.

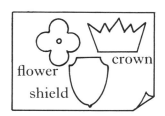
flower
crown
shield

2 Make a small cake of Plasticine, about the size of a 10p piece, but thicker, about 4 cm thick.

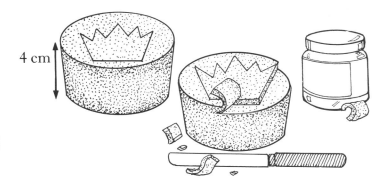
4 cm

3 Copy your design on to the top surface of the cake of Plasticine. Cut away the spare Plasticine all around your design.

4 Coat the surface of the Plasticine thinly with petroleum jelly.

5 Cut a strip of thin cardboard, about 2½ times as deep as the cake of Plasticine, and wrap it round the Plasticine. Fasten the end securely with sticky tape.

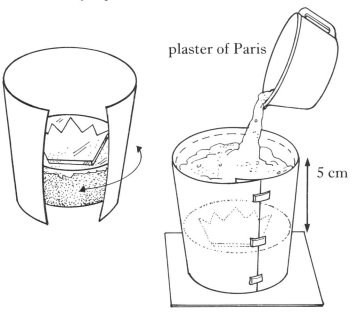
plaster of Paris
5 cm

6 Mix up some plaster of Paris with water according to the instructions on the packet.

7 Carefully pour it into the cardboard collar to a depth of about 5 cm. Tap it gently to remove air bubbles.

8 When the plaster of Paris is set, carefully remove the cardboard collar and separate the Plasticine from the plaster of Paris. Your seal is ready to use!

9 To use your seal, *either* find some more Plasticine (red and green would be the best colours to use; those were the colours of wax used for seals in the past) *or* get some sealing wax. If you choose to use sealing wax, you will need to melt it with a flame. **Do not do this without an adult to help you.**

10 If you are using Plasticine, then make another cake, about the size and thickness of a 10p piece. Carefully press your plaster of Paris seal down on to the Plasticine. You should see your own seal design on the Plasticine.

If you are using sealing wax, take a stick of sealing wax and **ask an adult** to light it for you. **Be careful**, the wax will get very hot as it melts and could burn your skin. Drop a small blob of melted wax a little bigger than your plaster of Paris seal on to a sheet of clean paper. While the wax is still runny, press your seal down into it gently but firmly, and remove it carefully. You should see a copy of your seal design set firmly into the wax.

At the time of Domesday Book, people fixed their seals on to documents using tags made of parchment. You could do the same.

You will need:
paper
scissors
sealing wax and matches **or**
Plasticine
your seal
an adult to help if you are using sealing wax

---

1 Take a sheet of paper. If you liked, you could write a letter on this first, either as yourself or pretending to be a lord who has just arrived in England with William the Conqueror. How would you describe your new village or town to your family back in France?

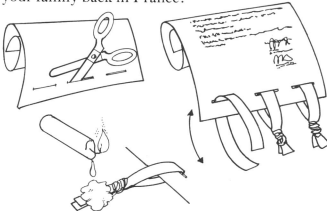

2 Carefully cut 2 or 3 slits at the bottom of the letter.

3 Cut 2 or 3 strips of paper, about 20 cm long and 3 cm wide. Thread them through the slits at the bottom of the letter.

4 Twist the ends of each strip together.

5 **If you have an adult to help you,** melt some more sealing wax over the ends of the strips, and use your plaster of Paris seal to press your own design into it.

If you do not have an adult to help you, make 2 cakes of Plasticine about the size of a 10p piece, press them together on either side of the strips of paper so that each strip is sandwiched between the Plasticine. Then press your plaster of Paris seal down on to the top cake of Plasticine. Your seal should be firmly fixed to your letter!

Project: Make a Quill Pen

Domesday Book was written by scribes using quill pens on parchment. The quill pens were made from goose feathers and the parchment was made from the specially-prepared skins of goats or sheep. It took over 500 sheep to provide all the parchment needed for the two volumes of Domesday Book. The ink was made from crushed oak galls (little growths that develop on oak twigs) and iron sulphate. Ink was often kept in inkwells made from the hollowed-out horns of cows or oxen. Scribes used a knife to trim their quill pens to a sharp point.

Writing with a quill pen or an old-fashioned 'dip-in' pen nib and holder is very much more difficult than using a felt-tip or biro. It is hard to keep the ink flowing smoothly. The scribes were obviously very skilful. There are very few blots or crossings-out in Domesday Book!

You can try to write like the Domesday scribes. Practise using a 'dip-in' pen nib and holder until you can write smoothly with it. You might find it helpful to draw various zig-zag patterns first, like this, before trying to write letters and whole words.

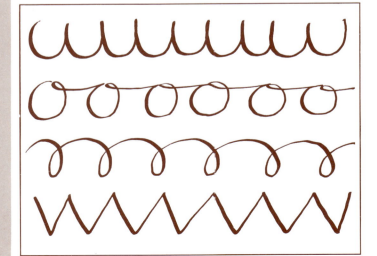

Look at the writing in the photograph of the Domesday Book text above. Try to copy the shapes of letters that the Domesday scribes used:

You can also try to make a quill pen, like the ones Domesday scribes used. You will need an adult to help you with some of the steps. **Do not try to harden or cut quills by yourself.**

First of all, you will need to find some goose feathers. You may be lucky enough to find these on a country walk, but more likely you will have to ask a grown-up to ask a butcher who sells poultry, or a farmer who keeps geese, for feathers for you.

Once you have found your quill feathers, make sure that they are clean. Wash them thoroughly using washing-up liquid, and dry them carefully. You could also use seagull feathers found on a beach, or pheasant or turkey feathers from a butcher.

Ask a grown-up to help you with the following steps:

1 Dip the tips of the quills in boiling water for about 30 seconds. This will harden them. Leave them to cool.

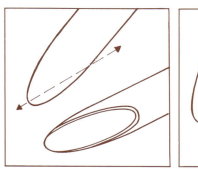 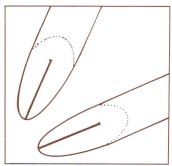

2 Ask a grown-up to slice the tips off the quills diagonally, using a sharp knife.

3 Then ask the grown up to make a small slit in the tips of the quill points.

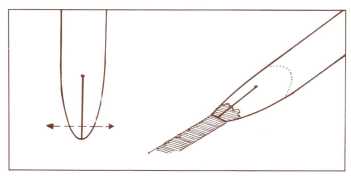

4 Finally, ask the grown up to cut a straight line across the tip of each quill. This will make a straight edge to write with.

Your quill pens are ready to use! Experiment to find the most comfortable way to hold them.

If you cannot find feathers to use, you can try to make a quill pen from different materials.

> **You will need:**
> quill toothpicks (you can buy these from a chemist) **or**
> plastic drinking straws
> sticky tape
> paper
> paint and brushes or felt tips
> scissors

1 Fasten the rounded end of the toothpick to one end of a drinking straw. Push one a little way inside the other if you can. Wind sticky tape around the join to make it firm and secure.

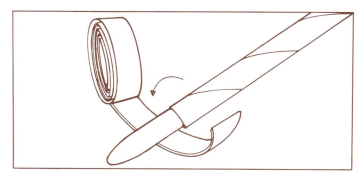

2 Using scissors, snip a tiny piece off the pointed edge of the quill, to make a straight edge to write with.

3 Draw a feather shape on paper. Make it about three-quarters as long as the drinking straw. Colour the feather shape and cut it out.

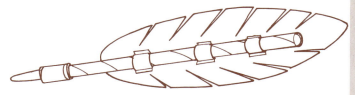

4 Using sticky tape, fasten the feather shape to the drinking straw, as shown in the drawing. Cut a fringe all round the feather shape. Your quill pen is ready to use. Now you will be able to see how difficult it must have been for the Domesday scribes to write so enormous a book so quickly and neatly!

5 If you cannot find quill toothpicks, use short pieces of plastic drinking straw. Cut them into the shape shown in the drawings above.

Project: Tapestry and Collage

The Bayeux Tapestry is a very large embroidered picture made at about the same time as Domesday Book. It tells the story of the Norman conquest of England in 1066. It is 70.4 metres long and 50 centimetres wide, and looks rather like a comic strip.

It was made on the orders of Bishop Odo of Bayeux, step-brother of William the Conqueror. It was embroidered by a group of nuns in Kent, and then taken to Bishop Odo's cathedral at Bayeux in France when it was finished.

English embroideries were highly-prized throughout Europe in the Middle Ages. The Bayeux Tapestry is very beautifully made, using woollen thread on a linen background. The colours have remained bright and clear for 900 years.

The embroidered pictures of the Tapestry tell us a great deal about the clothes, armour, ships, buildings and furniture belonging to the Normans. There is a commentary in Latin written alongside the pictures.

You could try to use some of the same embroidery stitches as the nuns of Kent used 900 years ago to make a smaller picture of a scene from your everyday life, your house or your pets. The pictures in the circles show you how.

First choose a subject for your picture. Don't chose anything too complicated! Draw the outline of your picture on paper, and mark on it what stitches you plan to use. Then use this as a chart to guide you while you are doing your embroidery.

Instead of embroidery, you could make a collage. Either choose a scene from the Norman Conquest, using pictures of the Bayeux Tapestry to help you, or else choose a scene from the daily life of your school. Imagine that someone will want to look at it in 900 years from now, like you are looking at pictures of the Bayeux Tapestry today.

Plan your collage project carefully with your friends, like the nuns of Kent planned the Tapestry. Divide your collage into sections and take one section each. Or take one subject each, and 'mass produce' cut-outs of trees, houses, tables, chairs etc. If you choose to make a collage picture of your classroom, you could ask every member of the class to paint or draw their own self portrait. (Use a mirror to look at while you draw yourself.) Arrange these self-portraits around tables or desks in the order in which people sit in the classroom. Add a border of various objects you can see in the classroom: books, bags, lunchboxes, pictures, plants, pets etc.

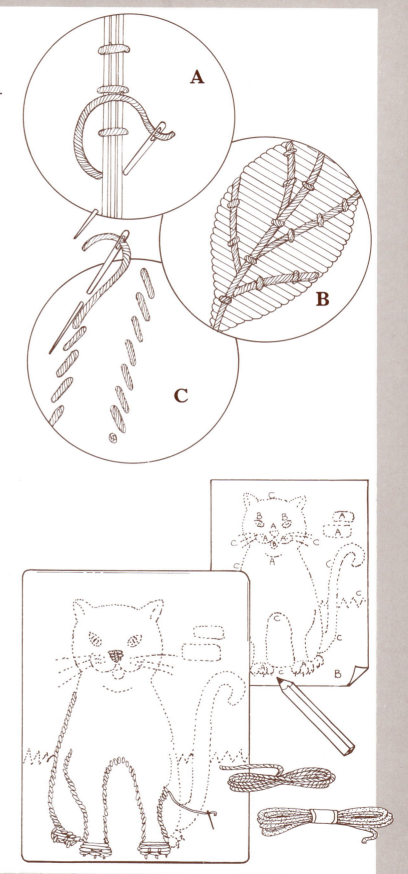

Project: Domesday Drama

Domesday Book and the Norman Conquest provide plenty of opportunities for drama activities based on their contents. The following topics suggest themselves:

* episodes from the Conquest of 1066 (using the story as depicted in the Bayeux Tapestry)
* the arrival of new Norman lords in a district and local opposition, perhaps incorporating the story of Hereward the Wake
* the arrival of the Domesday Commissioners in your neighbourhood, to check the progress of the survey

A second line of approach to Domesday Drama would be to plan a 'time-travel' exercise, to encourage the children to consider some of the differences between life now and in Domesday times. The photograph opposite shows a group of primary-age children acting out their own ideas of how Domesday villagers might feel in wintertime when food was running short, as part of a 'life in the countryside' drama exercise. Various 'then and now' contrasts could usefully be explored; food; housing; warfare; law and order; information gathering and processing; rich and poor.

A third possibility would be to hold a 'Domesday Day' with the whole class in costume, a simple meal (bread, water, vegetable 'pottage' for the poorer people; meat or cheese and 'wine' (fruit juice) for the lord and his retinue) at midday, and appropriate activities acted out (work in the fields, a trip to market, a session of the manor court, hunting and hawking etc.) The day might conclude with stories and songs in the 'great hall' of the lord's 'castle', with songs and stories from wandering minstrels. Costume can be improvised, as in the photograph opposite, from shawls, scarves, sheets and towels, or even sacking, worn over old teeshirts. Trousers can be 'cross-gartered' with string or tape to make leggings for boys; girls should wear long skirts if possible. More accurate costumes can be devised quite simply; see p. 46 for titles of useful books.

It would even be possible to use contemporary written evidence as a basis for drama activities. One of the most interesting survivals from the late Anglo-Saxon period is a short play in which various 'typical' characters – a ploughman, a shepherd etc. – describe their life and work. It is known as *Aelfric's Colloquy*, and was written by Aelfric, a monk from Cerne Abbas in Dorset. The play dates from around 995 A.D. Aelfric was in charge of the monastery school, and wrote the play as an aid to teaching Latin. Although it dates from almost a century before Domesday, it presents such a vivid and lively picture of everyday life that it is well worth considering for classroom use. Several modern translations are available; one is listed on p. 44. These tend to put accuracy of translation before dramatic subtlety, but the language could very easily be adapted for children to learn, or used as a basis for improvisation.

The format of Aelfric's play is of a schoolmaster questioning his pupils, each of whom takes the part of an adult with a particular role to play in society. The following extracts give some idea of the play's content and approach. Here is the schoolmaster, questioning the child who is pretending to be a monk:

MASTER: I ask you (*indicating a particular pupil*), what do you say to me? What is your work?

'MONK': I am a professed monk, and every day I sing seven times with the brethren, and I am busy with reading and singing, but nevertheless, between-times I want to learn to speak the Latin language.

MASTER: What do your friends do?

'MONK': Some are ploughmen, some shepherds, some oxherds; some huntsmen, some fishermen, some fowlers, some merchants, some shoe-makers, salters, bakers.

MASTER: What do you say, ploughman? How do you carry out your work?

'PLOUGHMAN': Oh, I work very hard, dear lord. I go out at daybreak driving the oxen to the field, and yoke them to the plough; for fear of my lord, there is no winter so severe that I dare hide at home; but the oxen, having been yoked and the share and coulter fastened to the plough, I must plough a full acre or more every day.

MASTER: Have you any companion?

'PLOUGHMAN': I have a lad driving the oxen with a goad, who is now also hoarse because of the cold and shouting.

MASTER: What else do you do in the day?

'PLOUGHMAN': I do more than that, certainly. I have to fill the oxen's bins with hay, and water them, and carry their muck outside.

MASTER: Oh, oh! It's hard work.

'PLOUGHMAN': It's hard work, sir, because I am not free.

Puzzle: Can you read Domesday Book?

Domesday Book is written in Latin, and the scribes used a form of shorthand, or code, for some common words to avoid writing them out in full over and over again. This saved space, and money too, because the parchment on which Domesday Book was written was very expensive. It also saved the scribes' time. Modern-day scribes have estimated that it took the men who copied out Domesday Book a whole day to write six pages.

Even if you do not know how to read Latin, you can still understand some of the Domesday text. This page will help you.

The first step in trying to understand any code is to try and decipher the alphabet that is being used. Look at the copy of a page from Domesday Book opposite, and then at the list of letters below. Try to copy out the Domesday way of writing letters opposite the modern forms of the letters. Some of the gaps have been filled in for you. You will see that some letters are almost the same today as they were 900 years ago; others have changed over the centuries.

A	J	S . . . . . .
B . ℬ, b	K	T . . 𝒯, ꞇ
C	L	U . . . . . .
D	M	V . . . . . .
E	N . ℕ, ꞑ	W . . . . .
F	O	X . . . . . .
G	P	Y . . . . . .
H . ꞕ, ꞗ	Q	Z . . . . . .
I	R	

Use the Domesday script to send a message to one of your friends. Can they read it?

Now see if you can read some whole words In the Domesday text opposite, some words are ringed. Using your alphabet, see whether you can read the words. The answers are given on p. 48.

Many of the words on the page opposite are written in shorthand, or code. Here are some of the shortened words, or abbreviations. Can you find examples of each type of abbreviation in the Domesday text opposite?

p^9 = *post* (or *postea*) ; meaning 'afterwards'

m^o = *modo*; meaning 'now'

$⁊$ = *et*; $\}$ meaning 'and'

Domesday scribes used Roman numbers to record how many men, pigs, acres of land etc. belonged to each manor. Here are the Roman numbers they used:

I	= 1	IX	= 9	L	= 50
II	= 2	X	= 10	LX	= 60
III	= 3	XI	= 11	LXXXX	= 90
IIII	= 4	XIX	= 19	C	= 100
V	= 5	XX	= 20	CC	= 200
VI	= 6	XXI	= 21	D	= 500
VII	= 7	XXXI	= 31		
VIII	= 8	XL	= 40		

Can you find the following numbers in the Domesday text opposite? Fill in the number of the line of text where you find the Roman numbers. One space has been filled in for you. Some answers are given on p. 48, but you will be able to find many other examples of Roman numbers on other lines too.

Roman 30 on line . . . .   Roman 400 on line . . . .
Roman 2 on line . . . .   Roman 7 on line . . . .
Roman 12 on line . . . .   Roman 8 on line . . . .
Roman 20 on line . . . .   Roman 29 on line . . . .
Roman 15 on line . . . .

Try, now, to see whether you can read a whole line of the text. Look at lines 22 and 23. They have been written out below, letter for letter, as in the original. Try to read the lines yourself, and then turn the page upside down to find out the answers. There is a translation of these two lines, to tell you what the shorthand Latin means, on p. 48.

ne 22: ⁊ Brundala iacet huic manerio XXX ac tre Tɴc I

ne 23: Car ⁊ II ac pti. Tɴc val XII lib p XXV lib blanc.

34

Line 1: ⁊ In Beretuna · vi · libi hoēs · xxx · aē t̄rę. Tnc · ii · car̄ · p̄

Line 2: ⁊ m̄ · i · ⁊ ii · aē p̄ti · ⁊ In Vroeham · ii · libi hoēs · lx aē t̄rę

Line 3: ⁊ ii · bord̄. Tnc · ii · car̄ · p̄ ⁊ m̄ · i · ⟨hoc ē⟩ totū inp̄tio de

Line 4: ettuna ʃ In Racheitha · iii · libi hoēs · iiii · car̄ t̄rę · ⁊ iii ·

Line 5: uilt · ⁊ xii · bord̄. tnc · iiii · ʃeru. Tnc · v · car̄ · p̄ ⁊ m̄ · iiii ·

Line 6: ⁊ vii · aē p̄ti. Tnc ual · xx · ʃot. m̄ · lx · ⁊ h̄t · i · leūg · in lon̄

Line 7: ⁊ viii · quar̄ in lat̄ · ⁊ xv · d de gelto · huic ⟨iacent⟩ ix · libi

Line 8: hoēs in Beretuna de · xl · aē · ʃemp · i · car̄ · ⁊ ʃūt in eodem

Line 9: p̄tio ⟨Rex⟩ ⁊ comes ʃocam · ⁊ Bretuna h̄t · dim̄ · leūg in

Line 10: lon̄g · ⁊ v · quar̄ in lato · ⁊ ⟨reddit⟩ · x · d · ingeldū regis ·

Line 11: ⌐ Ertincham ʃvd · Ɔ Eletham tenuit Guert · t · r · e ·

Line 12: xvi · car̄ t̄rę · Tnc · xx · uilt · p̄ ⁊ m̄ · xi · tnc ⁊ p̄ lxxxviii ·

Line 13: bord̄ · m̄ · lxv · tnc ⁊ p̄ · v · ʃ · m̄ · iii · Tnc vi · car̄ in dñio

Line 14: p̄ ⁊ m̄ · i · ⁊ vi · possunt fieri · xii · aē p̄ti · Tnc ⟨ʃilua⟩ cccc ·

Line 15: porc̄ · p̄ ⁊ m̄ · ccc ⟨ʃemp⟩ · ii · mot · ʃemp vii · porc̄ · ⁊ vi · ou

Line 16: ⁊ vii · cap · Tnc ⁊ p̄ lx · ʃoc · m̄ · xlvi · ⁊ h̄t · i · car̄ t̄rę · ⁊ dim̄

Line 17: ⁊ xiiii · bord̄ · Tnc xxx ⟨car̄⟩ p̄ ⁊ m̄ xxiiii · ⁊ viiii · aē p̄ti

Line 18: ʃilua · xii · por · ʃemp · ii · mot · ⁊ vi · car̄ ·

Line 19: huic man̄ iacet · i · berurta Sapedana · i · car̄ t̄rę · ⁊ ʃep

Line 20: iiii · uilt · Tnc · iii · bord̄ · p̄ ⁊ m̄ · ii · ʃemp · i · car̄ in dñio

Line 21: ⁊ ii · car̄ ⟨hom̄⟩ ⁊ dim̄ aē p̄ti · Silua · viii · porc̄ ·

Line 22: ⁊ Brundala iacet huic ⟨manerio⟩ xxx · aē t̄rę · Tnc · i ·

Line 23: car̄ · ⁊ ii · aē p̄ti · Tnc ual · xii · lib · p̄ · xxv · lib · blanc̄ ·

Line 24: m̄ · xx ix · lib · blancas · ⁊ xx · ʃot de gersuma · ⁊ h̄t · ii ·

Line 25: leūg · in lon̄g · ⁊ ii · in lat̄ · ⁊ xx · d ⟨de gelto⟩ huic v · libi hō·

Poetry and Prose

The Anglo-Saxon Chronicle for 1085 gives the immediate political context for the decision to compile Domesday Book. The Peterborough cleric who wrote the Chronicle entry for that year paints a grim picture:

In this year people said and declared for a fact, that Cnut, king of Denmark, son of King Sweyn, was setting out in this direction and meant to conquer this country with the help of Robert, count of Flanders, because Cnut was married to Robert's daughter. When William, king of England, who was then in Normandy – for he was in possession of both England and Normandy – found out about this, he went to England with a larger force of mounted men and infantry from France and Brittany than had ever come to this country, so that people wondered how this country could maintain all that army. And the king had all the army dispersed all over the country among his vassals, and they provisioned the army each in proportion to his land. And people had much oppression that year, and the king had the land near the sea laid waste, so that if his enemies landed, they should have nothing to seize on so quickly. But when the king found out for a fact that his enemies had been hindered and could not carry out their expedition – then he let some of the army go to their own country, and some he kept in this country over winter.

Then at Christmas, the king was at Gloucester with his council, and held his court there for five days, and then the archbishop and clerics had a synod for three days. There Maurice was elected bishop of London, and William for Norfolk and Robert for Cheshire – they were all the king's clerics.

After this, the king had much thought and very deep discussion with his council about this country – how it was occupied or with what sort of people. Then he sent his men over all England into every shire and had them find out how many hundred hides there were in the shire, or what land and cattle the king himself had in the country, or what dues he ought to have in twelve months from the shire. Also he had a record made of how much land his archbishops had, and his bishops and his abbots and his earls – and though I relate it at too great length – what or how much everybody was worth. So very narrowly did he have it investigated, that there was no single hide nor a yard of land, nor indeed (it is a shame to relate but it seemed no shame to him to do) one ox nor one cow nor one pig was there left out, and not put down in his record: and all these records were brought to him afterwards.

The following brief selection of poetry and prose is included in the hope that it may help teachers and others to answer the questions 'what was Domesday society like?' and 'how did people living then behave and think?'. It could also provide useful raw material to support drama or role-playing activities with children. Literary evidence not only offers us an insight into some of the leading figures in the Domesday story, but also into the values and beliefs of Anglo-Saxon and Norman society. Both cultures were, to a considerable extent, based on war, and in both, the warrior virtues of loyalty, courage and strength were highly valued. The Anglo-Saxon poem about the Battle of Maldon, for example, and the description of the drunken celebrations at a victory feast both demonstrate this. The Battle of Maldon poem also provides valuable information about Anglo-Saxon military tactics.

The Norman propaganda piece about the founding of the monastery on the site of the Battle of Hastings gives us a vivid picture of William the Conqueror as a war leader, and also reminds us of the importance attached by contemporaries to the place of the Church in their society. Even if, to a modern view, the idea of Duke William seeking divine approval for slaughter is hard to accept, the idea of a just war divinely rewarded with victory is a common theme in Anglo-Norman literature. Wulfstan's sermon accuses the pre-Conquest English of moral weakness; they are wicked and disloyal. The Norman Conquest could therefore be seen as divine punishment for their sins.

The description (on p.36) of the decision to compile Domesday Book shows the Norman government in action, and tells the story of the threatened Danish invasion which led to the extra tax being collected. This tax, in turn, was one of the reasons for compiling Domesday Book. This extract also shows the English reaction to the Domesday enquiry. The writer's sense that the whole process was a gross invasion of privacy still comes across strongly 900 years after the event!

Finally, the Anglo-Saxon riddles about writing are included as examples of a very common type of Anglo-Saxon poem. They tell us, perhaps rather unexpectedly, that the Anglo-Saxons enjoyed word-puzzles; they also give us a little more information, from the scribe's-eye view, about methods of writing and the value placed on books.

Criticism of the Anglo-Saxons from Archbishop Wulfstan's 'Sermon of the Wolf to the English', 1014

'Beloved men, recognize what truth is: the world is in haste and it is drawing near the end, and therefore the longer it is the worse it will get in the world. . . . . Understand properly also that for many years now the Devil has led this nation too far astray, and that there has been little loyalty among men although they spoke fair, and too many wrongs have prevailed in the land. . . . . daily they added one evil to another, and embarked on many wrongs and unlawful acts, all too commonly throughout the whole nation . . .'

A piece of Norman propaganda. From the Chronicle of Battle Abbey, founded on the site of the battle of Hastings by the Normans.

In the year 1066, the most noble William, duke of the Normans, sailed with a mighty army against England, so that he might wrest the realm of England, left by his kinsman king Edward, out of the grasp of the deceitful usurper Harold. . . . When Harold learned of the landing he marched against him with his army. The energetic duke faced him . . . at a place today called Battle. Now when the devout duke was armed in martial array, he called together his barons and knights and roused them all to fight faithfully in the battle, by his exhortation and by their hope in his promises. And in order to strengthen their hearts, he made before them and with the approval of all a vow to God, that if the divine mercy granted him victory over his enemies he would offer up that place to God, as wholly free and quit as he might be able to conquer it for himself. And there he would build a monastery, where servants of God might be brought together for the salvation of all, and especially those who should fall in that battle. It would be a place of sanctuary and help to all, paying back for the blood shed there by an unending chain of good works. His speech made the men more courageous; they entered the fight determinedly, and at last, as God had planned, on 14 October they won the victory: the duke's enemy lay fallen and his army fled. . . .

A description of the Normans written by the English monk William of Malmesbury in 1124.

They were then (in 1066), as now (1124), so elegantly attired as to arouse envy, at table epicures but not to excess. They are a race accustomed to war and almost unable to live without it. They attack the enemy readily, and, if force does not succeed, destroy by tricks and bribes. At home they build large at modest cost, envy equals, desire to outstrip superiors, and skin their subjects but protect them from others. They are faithful to their lords, but for a small offence quickly break faith; in misfortune they will consider treachery and for money change their mind. On the other hand they are the most kindly of all races and pay foreigners as much honour as their own; they marry into the conquered; and the rules of religion, which had died out in England, they revived by their coming. Everywhere you will see in the villages churches and in the towns monasteries going up in a new architectural style; and the country is so flourishing under the new customs that any nobleman would consider the day lost which he did not glorify with some splendid achievement.

Anglo-Saxon Riddles about Writing

Bookworm

I heard of a wonder, of words moth-eaten;
That is a strange thing, I thought; weird
That a man's song be swallowed by a worm,
His bound-up sentences, his bedside reading
Rustled in the night – and the robber-guest
Not one whit the wiser for the words he had munched!

A hand writing

I saw four fine creatures
Travelling in company; their tracks were dark,
Their trail very black. The bird that floats
In the air swoops less swiftly than their leader;
He dived beneath the wave. Drudgery it was
For the fellow that taught all four of them their ways
On their ceaseless visits to the vessel of gold.

A quill (excerpt)

. . . I catch in my mouth now
Black wood and water; my belly contains
Some dark thing that drops down upon me
As I stand here on my single foot.

The Saxon Chieftain at the Feast

. . . When the wine
Rose in him their chieftain roared and shouted
With triumph, bellowed so loud that his fierce
Voice carried far beyond
His tent, his wild pleasure was heard
Everywhere. And he demanded, over and over,
That his men empty their cups, drink deep.

Thus the evil prince, haughty
Giver of rings, soaked his soldiers
In wine, the whole day through,
drenched them till their heads swam
And they fell on the ground, all drunk;
lay as though death had struck them
Down, drained of their senses.

The Song of the Battle of Maldon
Extracts from the Anglo-Saxon poem which describes the Battle of Maldon, fought against the Danes in August 991.

The poem looks back rather nostalgically to the old heroic literary tradition, but gives a vivid picture of warfare at that time, and of the demands for Danegeld. The same battle tactics, e.g. the shield-wall, were used by the English at Hastings in 1066.

Its theme is loyalty to one's lord, to the death if need be. Survival means dishonour.

Then Brihtnoth (the war-leader, an earl,) began to array his men; he rode and gave counsel and taught his warriors how they should stand and keep their ground, bade them hold their shields aright, firm with their hands and fear not at all. When he had meetly arrayed his host, he alighted among the people where it pleased him best, where he knew his bodyguard to be most loyal.

Then the messenger of the Vikings stood on the bank, he called sternly, uttered words, boastfully speaking the seafarers' message to the earl, as he stood on the shore. 'Bold seamen have sent me to you, and bade me say, that it is for you to send treasure quickly in return for peace, and it will be better for you all that you buy off an attack with tribute, rather than that men so fierce as we should give you battle. There is no need that we destroy each other, if you are rich enough for this. In return for the gold we are ready to make a truce with you. If you who are richest determine to redeem your people, and to give to the seamen on their own terms wealth to win their friendship and make peace with us, we will betake us to our ships with the treasure, put to sea and keep faith with you.'

Brihtnoth lifted up his voice, grasped his shield and shook his supple spear, gave forth words, angry and resolute, and made him answer; 'Hear you, searover, what this folk says? For tribute they will give you spears, poisoned point and ancient sword, such war gear as will profit you little in battle. Messenger of the seamen, take back a message, say to your people a far less pleasing tale, how that there stands here with his troop an earl of unstained renown, who is ready to guard this realm, the home of Ethelred my lord, people and land; it is the heathen that shall fall in the battle. It seems to me too poor a thing that you should go with our treasure unfought to your ships, now that you have made your way thus far into our land. Not so easily shall you win tribute; peace must be made with point and edge, with grim battle-play, before we give tribute.' . . .

There, ready to meet the foe, stood Brihtnoth and his men. He bade them form the war-hedge with their shields, and hold their ranks stoutly against the foe. The battle was now at hand, and the glory that comes in strife. Now was the time when those who were doomed should fall. Clamour arose; ravens went circling, the eagle greedy for carrion. There was a cry upon earth.

They let the spears, hard as files, fly from their hands, well-ground javelins. Bows were busy, point pierced shield; fierce was the rush of battle, warriors fell on either hand, men lay dead . . .

(The earl is fatally wounded by a Viking spear:)

The earl looked up to heaven and cried aloud: 'I thank thee, Ruler of Nations, for all the joys that I have met with in this world. Now I have most need, gracious Creator, that thou grant my spirit grace, that my soul may fare to thee, into thy keeping, Lord of Angels, and pass in peace. It is my prayer to thee that fiends of hell may not entreat it shamefully.'

(The battle rages on; Brihtwold, an old warrior, is badly wounded, but he will not leave the fight:)

Brihtwold spoke and grasped his shield (he was an old companion); he shook his ash-wood spear and exhorted the men right boldly: 'Thoughts must be the braver, heart more valiant, courage the greater as our strength grows less. Here lies our lord, all cut down, the hero in the dust. Long may he mourn who thinks now to turn from the battle-play. I am old in years; I will not leave the field, but think to lie by my lord's side, by the man I hold so dear.'

The BBC Domesday Project

The BBC Domesday Project is making use of up-to-date technology to produce a contemporary portrait of Britain on interactive videodisc, i.e. a 1986 version of the original Domesday Book. Two videodiscs will be published at the end of 1986. One will present information compiled by schools and community groups, and will be known as the COMMUNITY disc. The other is the NATIONAL disc, which will contain information gathered by the Domesday Project researchers from national sources. Both videodiscs will illustrate almost every aspect of life in Britain in the 1980s through the use of maps, photographs, statistical surveys and text.

How the Videodisc Works

Anyone wanting to use the videodisc sits in front of a microcomputer and uses it to give commands to, or 'interact' with, a specially-designed Philips videodisc player. For example, if you chose to explore the COMMUNITY disc, you would type in the name of any place in the United Kingdom. The Ordnance Survey map of that place would appear on the screen and, if a school or community group has submitted a Domesday report on that place, you could also read the text and look at the photographs in its report. Over 14,000 schools and thousands of community groups have contributed Domesday reports on their local areas, recording what they think is important or interesting.

The NATIONAL disc: what will it contain?

The NATIONAL disc will represent the 'official' view of our time, drawing on material in public archives, government statistics, academic research studies, and photograph libraries. Users of the NATIONAL disc will have a very wide selection of information at their fingertips, displayed in graphically exciting ways. In answer to a user's enquiry, the videodisc would offer a 'menu' of pages of text, illustrations, data sets, photographs or clips of moving film which related to the chosen topic. Once the item was selected the user could 'interact' with the display to ask it to show precisely the information required. Graphs, charts, tables, could all be drawn and redrawn with minimal effort, feeding on a vast store of data in a way which has never before been possible.

The NATIONAL disc will also contain 'surrogate walks' which can take the disc user into and through almost any kind of environment, with the system selecting images from thousands of photographs taken from every angle. These walks will describe a variety of typical houses, a farm, a market town and areas of the countryside.

The COMMUNITY disc: how was the material collected?

The BBC sent out invitations to 33,000 schools in the United Kingdom, Isle of Man and the Channel Isles asking them to participate in the Domesday Project in the Summer Term of 1985. Co-ordinators in each LEA allocated all or part of a 4 × 3 km block to schools for survey, either on their own or in co-operation with other schools, community groups or individuals. The 14,000+ participating schools were sent a *Survey Guide*, a *Teacher's Handbook* which gave suggestions about how to derive the maximum educational benefit from the Project, a set of microcomputer software for recording the information to be sent to the BBC, and a return mailing pack.

What were the educational aims of participation in the Project?

The Domesday Project's aims were not only to collect data for this national survey but also to provide an educationally rewarding experience for the schools and community groups involved. Schools have reported on the following long-term educational aspects of participating in this national project.

Most of these activities can be used to make links between investigations of present-day conditions and events and life at the time of Domesday Book. Surveys, analysis of data, numeracy or report-writing assignments could all compare life 'then and now' using local materials and the original Domesday text.

environmental studies: many schools were able to continue or expand on work exploring their local environment and others realised the benefits of involving children more in their own surroundings. Children became much more aware of local concerns and issues.

survey methods: groups were asked to survey land cover and to count amenities for each square kilometre as well as writing text on life in their areas. Map-reading skills were developed. Teachers helped pupils to devise methods for analysing statistics. The problems of categorising data and the need for accuracy in record keeping were also explored.

interviews and questionnaires: children had to decide which information they needed, whom to interview, how to record, summarise and report the information. 'They became junior reporters,' commented one teacher, and were keen to pass on their news items to local newspapers.

writing: providing text suitable for a wide audience required the writing of several drafts, and extensive proof-reading. Some schools prepared a Domesday newspaper about their work, for distribution in the community. Some have found that the Domesday Project software is very useful for writing up other projects because it offers word processing facilities. Others have decided to invest in a word processor package for their microcomputers as the facility 'to make words appear on a television screen' offered significant help to pupils with language difficulties.

numeracy: children benefited in their fieldwork from being able to relate measurements such as '100 metres' or 'one square kilometre' to real examples. Some compared the amenities such as post offices and bus services in one square kilometre with another and were able to assess which area had better services.

pageants, plays, videos, slide/tape sequences: pageants recreated work done in compiling the original Domesday Book, or famous events in local history from the Domesday era. One pantomime from a Scottish school even comically portrayed the difficulties the Normans had in counting the lands and chattels of the Anglo-Saxons! Some schools made video or slide/tape records of their survey work which were shown to parents and groups in the community.

artwork and exhibitions: local scenes have been depicted in Bayeux-style tapestries for display in public buildings as a permanent record for the community; relief maps were made to provide a geographical reference; several schools working together on their 4 × 3 km block have presented a joint exhibition for display in each of the schools or in the local resource centre; participating schools in one LEA have contributed towards an LEA-wide exhibition; schools have exchanged visits to share their work.

Domesday Project resources available in 1986/7

Publications:
BBC Domesday Project Children's Book (working title), BBC Publications, 48pp, fully illustrated, £2.95, available Autumn 1986.
The *BBC Domesday Project Children's Book* compares the making of Domesday Book in 1086 with its 20th century counterpart on videodisc. How are such surveys used, what do they tell us about the land we live in and how has the land changed in the years in between?
Computers in Action Series, A & C Black, available Spring 1987.
One book in the *Computers in Action* series will look at how computers can help in surveys and at the BBC Domesday Project.

BBC Domesday System
The interactive videodisc system and the Domesday discs will be available by the end of 1986. A range of teachers' notes and software support for application in the curriculum will also be available. For further details please contact the Information Officer, BBC Domesday Project, BBC Offices, 54–58 Uxbridge Road, London W5 2ST.

Finding Out More

Primary Sources

Domesday Book. See pp. 12–13 for how to find the Domesday text for your own locality.

Alecto Historical Editions Ltd. are planning to issue a facsimile edition of the Great Domesday text in county volumes during 1986 and 1987. Enquiries may be made to them at 46 Kelso Place, London W8 5QG.

Domesday Satellites (other manuscripts associated with the making of Domesday Book). The texts of some of these are in print; for a discussion of these see H. Clarke, 'The Domesday Satellites', in P. Sawyer (ed.) *Domesday Book, a Reassessment*, London 1985.

English Historical Documents, vol.2 (1042–1189) ed. D.C. Douglas and G.W. Greenaway, London 1959, prints translations of the most important source materials for this period, including the Anglo-Saxon Chronicle, and several entries from Domesday Book itself.

The Bayeux Tapestry has been photographed and published in several modern editions. Two versions which should be widely available are those edited by C. Gibbs-Smith, London 1973, and Sir F. Stenton, London 1965. A new, de-luxe edition, prepared from recent photographs, has just been published, edited by D. Wilson, London 1985.

A document collection concerning the Norman Conquest is also available: R. Allen Brown, *The Norman Conquest; Documents of English History* series, No. 5, 1984.

Treating old material in a new way is: Thomas Hinde, *Domesday Book, England's Heritage, Then and Now*, London 1985. A new book, designed to coincide with the 900th anniversary of Domesday's compilation. A gazetteer, contrasting Domesday material with descriptions of present-day villages and towns.

General Background Reading

H.R. Loyn, *Anglo-Saxon England and the Norman Conquest*, London 1966. A book which has introduced thousands of undergraduates to the study of the Anglo-Saxon world.

E. Miller and J. Hatcher, *Medieval England Rural Society and Economic Change 1086–1348*, Longman 1978.

M.M. Postan, *The Medieval Economy and Society*, London 1972. A simple introduction to the period by a very authoritative historian.

M.T. Clanchy, *England and its Rulers*, London 1984. An overview of the political and constitutional history of the period.

S. Reynolds, *An Introduction to the History of English Medieval Towns*, Oxford 1977. A helpful guide to this important topic.

R.I. Page, *Life in Anglo-Saxon England*, London 1960. A good introduction to the beliefs and culture of the period.

Local Studies

A great many local studies of Domesday material have been published in local historical and archaeological journals. These studies can often prove helpful in shedding light on particular local problems of interpretation. A list of books and articles on individual counties and towns published before 1962 is printed in R. Welldon Finn, *An Introduction to Domesday Book*, London 1963. A more up to date list is given in the 3rd edition of H.C. Darby's *Domesday geography of eastern England*, 1971.

Specialist works on Domesday Studies

F.W. Maitland, *Domesday Book and Beyond*,
Cambridge 1897.
The classic book on the subject. Nearly 90 years old and still the best.

J.H. Round, *Feudal England*, London 1895.
A controversial book, still debated. Round was was an outspoken and influential figure during his lifetime. Many of his views have been rejected by recent historians. See, for example, Macdonald and Snooks, below.

R. Lennard, *Rural England*, 1086–1135, Oxford 1959.
An important but rather difficult book. It looks in great detail at the conditions in the countryside in the years following the Domesday survey.

E. King, 'Domesday Studies', *History*, 58, 1973 pp. 403–9.
A useful review article, summarising different views about the purpose and nature of Domesday studies.

V.H. Galbraith, *The Making of Domesday Book*, Oxford 1961.
The most helpful study of how Domesday Book was compiled.

S. Harvey, 'Domesday Book and its Predecessors', *English Historical Review*, 86, 1971, pp. 753–73.
Argues that Domesday Book was based upon pre-existing taxation assessment records, now lost. Also a useful introduction to recent research.

J. Macdonald and G. Snooks, 'Were the Tax Assessments of Domesday Book Artificial?' *Economic History Review*, 2nd. Series, 38, no. 3, 1985, pp. 352–372.
An article advancing a new theory; that geld was assessed not on hides or ploughlands, but on the total value of each manor.

P. Sawyer, *Domesday Book, a Reassessment*, London 1985.
An important new collection of essays by many of the leading Domesday historians.

The Domesday Geography of England Series

A pioneering attempt to analyse the Domesday evidence on a regional basis, allowing comparisons to be made between different parts of the countryside, and an overall picture of topics such as Domesday population or livestock to be obtained. Very helpful as a guide to the interpretation of local Domesday material.

H.C. Darby, *The Domesday geography of eastern England*, 3rd. edition, Cambridge 1971

H.C. Darby and I.B. Terret (eds), *The Domesday geography of midland England*, 2nd. edition, Cambridge 1971

H.C. Darby and E.M.J. Campbell (eds) *The Domesday geography of south-east England*, Cambridge 1962

H.C. Darby and I.S. Maxwell (eds), *The Domesday geography of northern England*, Cambridge 1962

H.C. Darby and R. Welldon Finn (eds), *The Domesday geography of south-west England*, Cambridge 1967

H.C. Darby and G.R. Versey, *Domesday Gazetteer*, Cambridge 1975.

H.C. Darby, *Domesday England*, Cambridge 1977.

Landscape History

A useful introduction to the study of the Domesday landscape is A. Rogers and T. Rowley, *Landscapes and Documents*, London 1974. See also T. Rowley and M. Aston, *Landscape Archaeology, an introduction to fieldwork techniques in post-Roman landscapes*, Newton Abbot 1974 and T. Rowley, *The Norman Heritage 1059–1200*, London 1982.

An excellent introduction to landscape history and local history in general is W.G. Hoskins, *Local History in England*, 2nd. edition, London 1972.

Literature
A good guide to late Anglo-Saxon and Anglo-Norman literature is M. Alexander, *Old English Literature*, London 1983.
Useful collections of medieval literature are given in B. Stone, *Medieval English Verse*, Harmondsworth 1964 and B. Ford (ed.), *The New Pelican Guide to English Literature Vol. 1, Part 1*, Harmondsworth 1982.

Domesday Drama
The test of *Aelfric's Colloquy* can be found in E. Swanton, *Anglo-Saxon Prose*, London 1960.

Domesday Book and the Computer
Three separate projects to computerise some or all of the Domesday text are in progress at the moment. Two are discussed in J. Palmer, 'Domesday Book and the Computer' in P. Sawyer, *Domesday Book; a Reassessment*, London 1985 (the Hull Data Base and the Santa Barbara Computer Project); a third is mentioned in J. Macdonald and G. Snooks, 'Were the Tax Assessments of Domesday England Artificial?' *Economic History Review*, 2nd series, 38, 1985, pp. 352–372, (the Flinders University Project).

Records of Medieval Music
Little secular music survives from the Domesday period, but the following 300 years are well represented on records. The following form a good introduction to the music of the period:

Instruments of the Middle Ages and the Renaissance
EMI SLS 998(2)
Music of the Crusades
Argo ZRG 673
Elegies for Kings and Princes
Harmonia Mundi HMF 237
A Medieval Christmas
Nonesuch H71 315
Music of the Gothic Era
ARCHIV 2723 045 (3)

Audio-Visual Teaching Materials
Filmstrips
The following make extensive use of original sources:
S.M. Newton, *Looking into History* series,
1. *The Bayeux Tapestry I*
2. *The Bayeux Tapestry II*
3. *England at the time of the Conquest*.
They can be very easily cut up and mounted for use in the same way as conventional slides.

The Bodleian Library in Oxford has published a very large number of the illuminated medieval manuscripts in its collections in filmstrip form. They can be ordered from VP Filmstrips, The Green, Northleach, Cheltenham, GL54 3EX Although they mostly date from the centuries immediately following the compilation of Domesday Book, these illustrations give a vivid picture of everyday life not vastly different from life in Domesday times. An illustrated catalogue is available, and filmstrips may be ordered by post from the Publications Officer, Clarendon Building, Bodleian Library, Oxford OX1 3BG.

The following filmstrips contain splendid collections of manuscript illustrations on selected themes:

Roll 251.6	Anglo-Saxon Illustration
Roll 175H	English Rural Life
Roll 151A/B	The Labours of the Months
Roll 162D	Domestic Equipment
Roll 145C	Medieval Food
Roll 164D	Warfare
Roll 164E	Transport
Roll 163C	Costume
Roll 164B	Towns
Roll 162B(4)	Children
Roll 162B(1)	Games and Toys

Posters and Maps
Three posters, The Norman Conquest, The Medieval Town, and Medieval Castles, can be obtained from Pictorial Charts Educational Trust, 27 Kirchen Road, London W13 0UD.

Domesday posters, maps, wallcharts and scrolls can be ordered from Garnons Williams Publications, Hardwicke Stables, Hadnall, Shrewsbury, SY3 4AS. A descriptive list is available.

Recommended Children's Books about Domesday Book and Anglo-Norman England

Suitable for the 8–12 age range.

Peter Boyden, *The Children's Book of Domesday England*, Kingfisher/English Tourist Board 1985.
Divided into three sections: What is Domesday Book? How Domesday Book was Compiled; Domesday England. Attractive, with lively artwork and some photographs. Comprehensive, detailed text might be difficult for some under 12s to read. Recommended.

N. Denny and J. Filmer-Sankey, *The Bayeux Tapestry*, Collins 1966, reprinted 1985.
Takes the reader step-by-step through the events leading up to the Norman invasion, and the day of the Battle of Hastings, using the strip-cartoon approach adopted by the Tapestry itself. Illustrated with photographs of the Tapestry. Short text suitable for readers of 9 and above. Highly recommended as accessible source material.

BBC TV Zig-Zag *Book of the Normans*, Heritage Books/Longman 1983.
A determinedly populist approach adopted here; history as entertainment! But the information, presented in comic strips and puzzle pictures, is clearly put across in a way likely to catch the reader's attention. Songs and projects, too.

G. Thie, *Living in the Past, the Middle Ages*, Basil Blackwell 1983.
Another book designed to involve the reader. Simple text, large illustrations (mostly from manuscripts) documentary extracts and 'things to do' suggestions for follow-up work.

H. Scarry, *Looking into the Middle Ages*, Hodder and Stoughton 1984.
The pop-up approach to history! Clever paper engineering presents views 'into' the past. We can see inside a castle, a cathedral etc. Text minimal and not always very accurate, and the pop-up pictures are non-specific as to country and century. But a useful talking point, with a fascination all of its own.
More accurate are D. Macaulay *Castle*, Collins 1977 and *Cathedral*, Collins 1982.

Roy Burrell, *The Oxford Children's History, Vol. 1*, Oxford 1983.
Perhaps the best-known junior-level textbook for this period. Has narratives of the Conquest, explanations of castle-building, and a spread on the making of Domesday Book.

Four books in the well-known *Peoples of the Past* series cover this period. The title on the Normans deals with the events of the Conquest and the making of Domesday Book itself. The others provide background. All are illustrated with photographs of contemporary objects or illustrations, plus accurate reconstruction artwork:
T. Triggs, *The Saxons*, Macdonald Educational 1979
M. Gibson, *The Vikings*, Macdonald Educational 1976
P. Rooke, *The Normans*, Macdonald Educational 1977
F. Macdonald, *The Middle Ages*, Macdonald Educational 1984

G. Caselli, *The Roman Empire and the Dark Ages*, *History of Everyday Things* series, Macdonald 1981. Accurate and very attractive reconstruction drawings showing how many 'everyday things' worked. Despite its title, covers the Anglo-Norman period. Text suitable for 10+ range.

N. Scarfe, *Norman England*, in the *Focus on History* series, Longman 1976.
Simply-written and well illustrated using many photographs of primary sources.

The *History 11–13* series being published by Holmes-McDougall will include a title on *The Battle of Hastings* as a "Level 2" study in evidence. This series incorporates the Schools History Project's approach of focusing learning on four key concepts, of which evidence is one. It is due to appear in 1986.

Children's Fiction

Two classic children's stories describe the Conquest and its aftermath:
Rosemary Sutcliff, *Shield Ring*, Oxford University Press 1956.
Charles Kingsley, *Hereward the Wake*, Macmillan 1874.

Teachers' Materials
The Public Record Office, in association with the Daily Telegraph and Prudential Assurance, have produced a *Teachers' Pack* to accompany their *Domesday* exhibition to be held during 1986. It is designed for use with primary and middle school age children. It can be ordered from Mrs Susan Lumas, Public Record Office, Chancery Lane, London WC2A 1LA

A *Teachers' Pack* has also been produced to accompany the Winchester *Domesday 900* exhibition. It can be ordered from Mr Alan Bates, Domesday Exhibition Office, City Offices, Guildhall, Winchester.

There is a Domesday *Special Issue* of *Junior Education* (No. 24, 1986) with many suggestions for classroom work based on Domesday Book. Useful material, and two splendid posters, can also be found in two back issues of *Junior Education*, 'Saxons' (May 1984) and 'Medieval Village' (September 1985). All can be ordered from Subscriptions Dept., Scholastic Publications, Westfield Road, Southam, Leamington Spa, Warwicks, CV33 0JH.

A role-play pack for use with schoolchildren, *Our Domesday Village*, has been developed by the Education for Neighbourhood Change group at the University of Nottingham, and will be for publication in April 1986. Enquiries to: Education for Neighbourhood Change, University of Nottingham, University Park, Nottingham, NG7 2RD.

A pamphlet, J. Fines, *Domesday in the Classroom*, was published by Phillimore in 1982.

Costume Reference
J. Cassin-Scott, *Costumes and Settings for Historical Plays*: vol. 2, *The Medieval Period*, Batsford 1979.
D. Yarwood, *Outline of English Costume*, Batsford 1967.
M. Sichel, *History of Children's Costume*, Batsford 1983.

Places to Visit
Domesday Book itself is housed in the Public Record Office, Chancery Lane, London WC2A 1LA. It will be on display in the museum there during 1986.

For information about a special Domesday exhibition to be held between April and September 1986 contact Mr J. Watkins, Domesday Bookings, Public Record Office, at the address above. Telephone 01 405 0741.

There will be a special *Domesday 900* exhibition in the Great Hall, Winchester, from Easter until the end of October 1986, organised by the *Sunday Times*, Hampshire County Council, and Winchester City Council.

Domesday Stop Press
Many publishers are planning to bring out books on Domesday topics during 1986. The following titles are all for adults:
E. M. Hallam, *The Domesday Book through Nine Centuries*, Public Record Office, London
(various authors) *Domesday Heritage*, Arrow Publications
The National Domesday Anniversary Committee, *Domesday – 900 years of England's Norman Heritage*, Millbank Publications
J. Ravensdale, *The Domesday Inheritance*, Souvenir
(various authors) *Domesday Revisited: A Traveller's Guide*, Severn House

A group of children from Sapperton Junior School in Gloucestershire have studied the life of their village for the past five years. Their findings are reported in *Village Heritage*, published by Alan Sutton. The book is introduced by television historian Michael Wood.

Television
As well as the BBC Domesday Project programmes and teaching materials (see p. 40), there will also be a BBC TV series, to be broadcast during Autumn 1986 in which Michael Wood will be discussing Domesday Book and related topics.

Index

Answers

ANSWERS TO WORDSQUARE PUZZLE

S	Q	M	E	A	D	O	W	W	W O O D	J
T	V	R	P	D E M E S N E	F	E	O
M I L L	O	K	A	B	W	P	E	R	F	X
A	L	O	Z	M A N O R	A	O	E	I	E
P	L	R	S	E	M	O	R	E	S	P	E	S	N
G E L D	S	Q	R	D	D	T	L	M	H	Z
A	I	H I D E	T	A	W	U	O	A	E	P
B	N	S L A V E	R	E	R	U	N	R	L
M	Z	I	S	Y	C A C R E	G	M	Y	O
C O T T A R	B	F	D	T	H	F	J	U
T	N	S O K E M A N	B	A	E	L	G
W I L L I A M	H A R O L D	H

* tenant of manor — villein
* grass grown for hay — meadow
* lots of trees — wood
* lord's home farm — demesne
* grinds corn — mill
* tax — geld
* the book of 1086 — Domesday Book
* estate with tenants — manor
* area for tax collecting — hide
* man owned by another — slave
* the amount of land that could be ploughed in a day — acre
* man with a cottage and a little land — cottager/cottar
* where animals graze — pasture
* tool used to prepare land before sowing corn — plough
* not a slave — freeman
* the conqueror — William
* King defeated at Hastings — Harold
* this man sounds as if he's got rather wet! — sokeman

ANSWERS TO 'CAN YOU READ DOMESDAY?' PUZZLE

Ringed words:

line 3	hoc est	means 'this is'
line 7	iacent	means 'belongs to'
line 9	Rex	means 'king'
line 10	reddit	means 'pays rent'
line 14	silva	means 'wood'
line 15	semp (semper)	means 'always'
line 17	car (caruca)	means 'plough'
line 21	hom (homines)	means 'men'
line 22	manerio	means 'manor'
line 25	gelto	means 'geld'

Roman numbers:

30 on line 1
2 on line 2
12 on line 5
20 on line 6
15 on line 7
400 on line 14
7 on line 16
8 on line 21
29 on line 24

Lines 22–23

Line 22 And Brundale belongs to this manor. (It contains) 30 acres of land. Then one

Line 23 plough and 2 acres of meadow. Then it was worth £12, (and) afterwards £15 of silver.

48